I0748862

Transactions
of the
American Philosophical Society
Held at Philadelphia
For Promoting Useful Knowledge
Vol. 88, Part 3

THE QUEEN OF SICILY

AND GOTHIC STAINED GLASS IN MUSSY AND TONNERRE

Meredith Parsons Lillich

American Philosophical Society
Independence Square ❖ Philadelphia
1998

ISBN:0-87169-883-8
US ISSN: 0065-9746

Library of Congress Cataloging-in-Publication Data

Lillich, Meredith P., 1932-
The Queen of Sicily and Gothic stained glass in Mussy and Tonnerre / Meredith Parsons Lillich.
p. cm. -- (Transactions of the American Philosophical Society, ISSN 0065-9746 ; vol. 88, pt. 3)
Includes bibliographical references and index.
ISBN 0-87169-883-8
1. Glass painting and staining, Gothic--France--Mussy-sur-Seine--Themes, motives. 2. Glass painting and staining--France--Mussy-sur-Seine--Themes, motives. 3. Glass painting and staining, Gothic--France--Tonnerre--Themes, motives. 4. Glass painting and staining--France--Tonnerre--Themes, motives. 5. Marguerite, de Bourgogne, Queen, consort of Charles I, King of Naples, ca. 1249-1308--Art patronage. 6. Saint-Pierre-ès-Liens (Church : Mussy-sur-Seine, France) 7. Hôpital Notre Dame des Fontenilles. I. Title. II. Series: Transactions of the American Philosophical Society ; v. 88, pt. 3.
NK5349.M87L56 1998
748.594'331--dc21 98-20435
CIP

TABLE OF CONTENTS

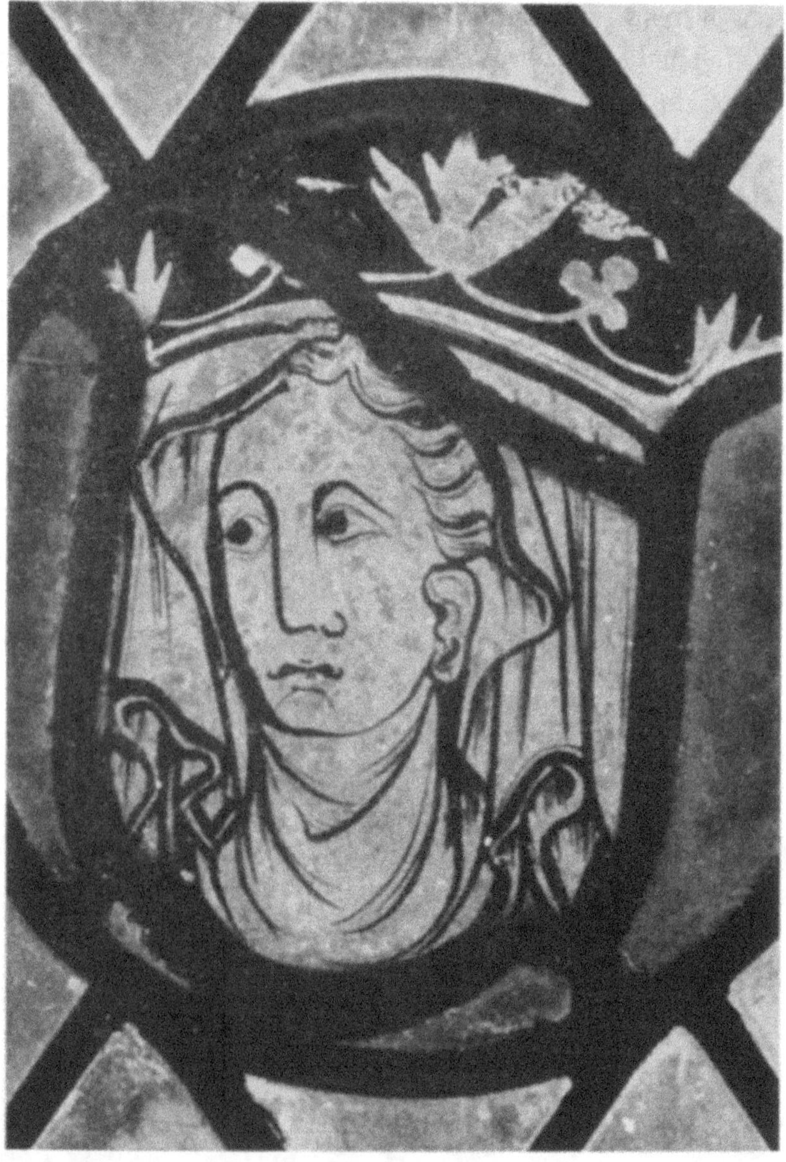

Frontispiece. Marguerite de Bourgogne, Queen of Sicily. Tonnerre, ca. 1293-95. Inventory no. 1. (after *Société d'archéologie et d'histoire du Tonnerrois, Bulletin annuel* 1973).

For Suzanne Sulzberger
(1903-1990)

Illustrations

PREFACE

Following the death of St Louis, a new court fashion of ostentatious display was introduced into French stained glass with the advent of Queen Marie de Brabant, who in 1274 became the second wife of St Louis' heir Philippe le hardi. Little stained glass in this new style survives, since the very motifs that made it different—large donor 'portraits,' elaborate heraldry, lavish name-inscriptions—became the most attractive targets of vandalism during the Hundred Years' War, the Franco-Burgundian struggles of the fifteenth century, the Huguenot conflict thereafter, and finally the French Revolution. This study reconstructs two ensembles in what might be called the 'new court style,' at the collegiate church of Mussy-sur-Seine in southern Champagne and at the famous medieval hospital of Tonnerre in Burgundy (see map Fig. 1). Both of them can be directly connected with the extraordinary figure of Marguerite de Bourgogne.

Burgundian princess, second wife and then widow of Charles d'Anjou, St Louis' brother, and titled the Queen of Sicily, Marguerite was a great peacemaker and one of the most revered agents of Christian charity of the Gothic era. Scholars have long recognized, on the basis of firm documentation, that she constructed the *Hôtel-Dieu* of Tonnerre from 1293 to 1295 and then retired to live adjoining it, to serve the sick and needy for the remainder of her life.

Mussy, on the other hand, has been dated in the late 1290s and attributed to the patronage of Guillaume de Mussy, corrupt agent of Philippe le Bel. He had nothing to do with it. In this study, the correct date is demonstrated to be around 1288, when the Queen of Sicily was peacemaking a violent disturbance at Mussy. She is connected here with Mussy in scholarship for the first time.

The Mussy windows (Fig. 2) can be reconstructed almost completely with evidence from the surviving images, archival data, early photographs and drawings, stylistic analysis, and careful identification of the heraldry and inscriptions. This study presents the following identifications. Bay 102 was a gift of Gui de Genève, bishop of Langres, whose summer residence was at Mussy and who was a party to the disturbance; gifts were contributed by his grandnieces in the family of Vienne and by Jean de Rochefort, who was to succeed him as bishop; Bay 104 was donated by the mason Perrinet Barottier (here identified as the designer of Mussy and Tonnerre) and his wife Jacquette; Bay 103 was a memorial to Gui de Mussy, soldier of Charles d'Anjou in Naples and undoubtedly killed in the Sicilian Vespers massacre of 1282.

Finally, the Queen contributed Bay 100 (the Crucifixion), Bay 0 beneath it (the local St Vallier, patron of her parish at her residence in Tonnerre) and possibly Bay 101—totally destroyed but probably adorned with crowned images of Marguerite and Charles d'Anjou and their heraldry, as in 600 examples known from the windows of the hospital of Tonnerre. I propose that Marguerite de Bourgogne, queen of Sicily,—who upon being widowed in 1285 left Naples and returned to the land of her birth—found the architect and glaziers for her grand hospital project of the 1290s while serving as peacemaker in Mussy.

This study was written on a research leave from Syracuse University (1994), based on research made possible by grants from the American Philosophical Society (1990) and the National Endowment for the Humanities (1990), and a fellowship at the Institute for Advanced Study in Princeton (1988). I am extremely grateful for their support, as well as for continuing kindnesses of Elizabeth A.R. Brown, Michael Cothren, Terryl Kinder, and many French archivists and conservators whom I have endeavored to thank in appropriate footnotes.

PART I

MUSSY-SUR-SEINE AND THE PROBLEM OF ITS DONOR

The apse of the Gothic church of Saint-Pierre-ès-Liens in Mussy-sur-Seine (Aube)—Mussy-l'Evêque until the Revolution—contains an ensemble of stained glass of great beauty and, as has not been realized, equally great social interest.[1] The lower row of windows presents unusual blankglazing (unpainted grisailles often associated with early Cistercian churches) while the clerestories above are glazed with band windows, that is, with a colored band of figures sandwiched *en litre* between painted-foliage grisailles above and below (Fig. 3). Three coats of arms, none indisputably identified, survive, as well as one enigmatic inscription. The range of color is limited and brilliant, dominated by vivid primaries and opaque white. The strong painting achieves a remarkable focus, with passages of expressionistic exaggeration. There is no silver stain. The dating, which in the absence of documentation has been based solely on style, has ranged around 1300.

In its border region of southern Champagne, Mussy has found no ready comparison. Both architecture and glass routinely have been considered a belated, rural, simplified version of the prestigious church of Saint-Urbain de Troyes, a 1262 foundation of Pope Urbain IV. The resemblance, however, is superficial and the comparison unsatisfactory. Branner called Mussy "the final Burgundian design of the century," noting a family resemblance to Saint-Thibault-en-Auxois (ca. 1290-1320) and relating the austerity of its smooth unmolded surfaces to Saint-Bénigne at

[1] The Mussy glass has been catalogued recently in *Les Vitraux de Champagne-Ardenne*, Corpus Vitrearum France, Recensement IV (Paris: 1992) pp. 146-49, with bibliography. I would like to thank Isabelle Balsamo for access to this work before publication. I am indebted to the late Jean-Michel Musso, Architecte en chef des Monuments historiques, for facilitating my access to the monument in 1990; I am also grateful to Anne Pinto for permission to consult her master's thesis and to Anne Prache for making a copy available to me ("Les Vitraux de l'abside de Mussy-sur-Seine," Mémoire de maîtrise, Université de Paris IV, 1985). My work was supported by a fellowship at the Institute for Advanced Study, Princeton (fall 1988) and by grants from the National Endowment for Humanities and the American Philosophical Society (1990).

Dijon (1281-after 1300).[2] Jean Bony included Mussy in his discussion of "The Northern Edges of Burgundy," underlining similarities of detail (triplet tracery pattern, plain champfered arches, continuous order without capitals; cf. Figs. 3-4, 10, 51-52) to English traditions first appearing in Cistercian building in Yorkshire.[3] More significant to the present study is Francis Salet's suggestion that the architect of Mussy may have built the Hôpital at Tonnerre (Yonne), some fifty kilometers southwest and firmly dated 1293-95.[4] (See map Fig. 1.) Mussy was in the county of Tonnerre, both Mussy and Tonnerre were in the former diocese of Langres (Haute-Marne), and Mussy was the site of the bishop's summer residence. Established by the bishop, at the request of the parish, in 1218, the collegiate church of Mussy was totally replaced in an undocumented campaign at the end of the same century.

From the seventeenth through nineteenth centuries, the building and glazing of Mussy were attributed to Gilles Vignier, imaginary crusader who lived only in the fanciful family genealogy concocted by the Jesuit Jacques Vignier (1603-69). Jacques was cousin to the proven text-forger Père Jérôme Vignier (1606-61), whose lies gave birth during his lifetime to the saying, "les vérités du Père Vignier."[5] The phrase could as easily

[2] Robert Branner, *Burgundian Gothic Architecture* (London: 1960) pp. 99, 156. Whether Mussy is to be aligned with Champagne or Burgundy is not the point here, "les limites de la Champagne et de la Bourgogne étant particulièrement imprécises" in the words of Gaston Saffroy, *Bibliographie généalogique, héraldique et nobiliaire de la France* II (Paris: 1970) p. 209. He lists Tonnerre, for example, under Champagne (pp. 211, 229).

[3] Jean Bony, *French Gothic Architecture of the 12th and 13th Centuries* (Berkeley: 1983) pp. 437-45. From 1274-84 Champagne was administered from Troyes by Edmund Crouchback, King Henry III's second son, who was married to Blanche d'Artois, widow of the last count of Champagne (p. 440); see also Francis Salet, "L'Eglise de Mussy-sur-Seine," *Congrès archéologique* CXIII (1955) pp. 327-28.

[4] Francis Salet, "L'Hôpital Notre-Dame des Fontenilles à Tonnerre," *Congrès archéologique* CXVI (1958) p. 233. I would, however, reverse his proposed chronology of Tonnerre first and Mussy to follow.

[5] Nicolas Bourbon (the younger), *Borboniana*, ch. V, published in v. II of François Bruys (1708-38), *Mémoires historiques, critiques, et littéraires*, ed. Philippe-Louis Joly (Paris: 1751) p. 251: "Il y a céans un certain Père, qui autrefois a été Huguenot, nommé le Père Vignier, qui est un grand, excellent & hardi menteur. D'où on dit par ironie: *Les Vérités du Père Vignier, les Promenades de M. de Bourbon, la Science du Père Gomer, la Conscience du Père Bonnet.*" See also: René Kerviler, "La Champagne à l'Académie française. II. Nicolas Bourbon (1574-1644)," *Revue de Champagne et de Brie* III (1877) p. 416; Abbé Roussel, "Chronique," *Revue de Champagne et de Brie* X, 2e semestre (1880) p. 139. On Jérome Vignier's forgeries see Julien Havet, "Questions mérovingiennes. II. Les découvertes de Jérome Vignier," *Bibliothèque de l'Ecole des chartes* XLVI (1885) pp. 205-71 and XLVII (1886) pp. 335-41.

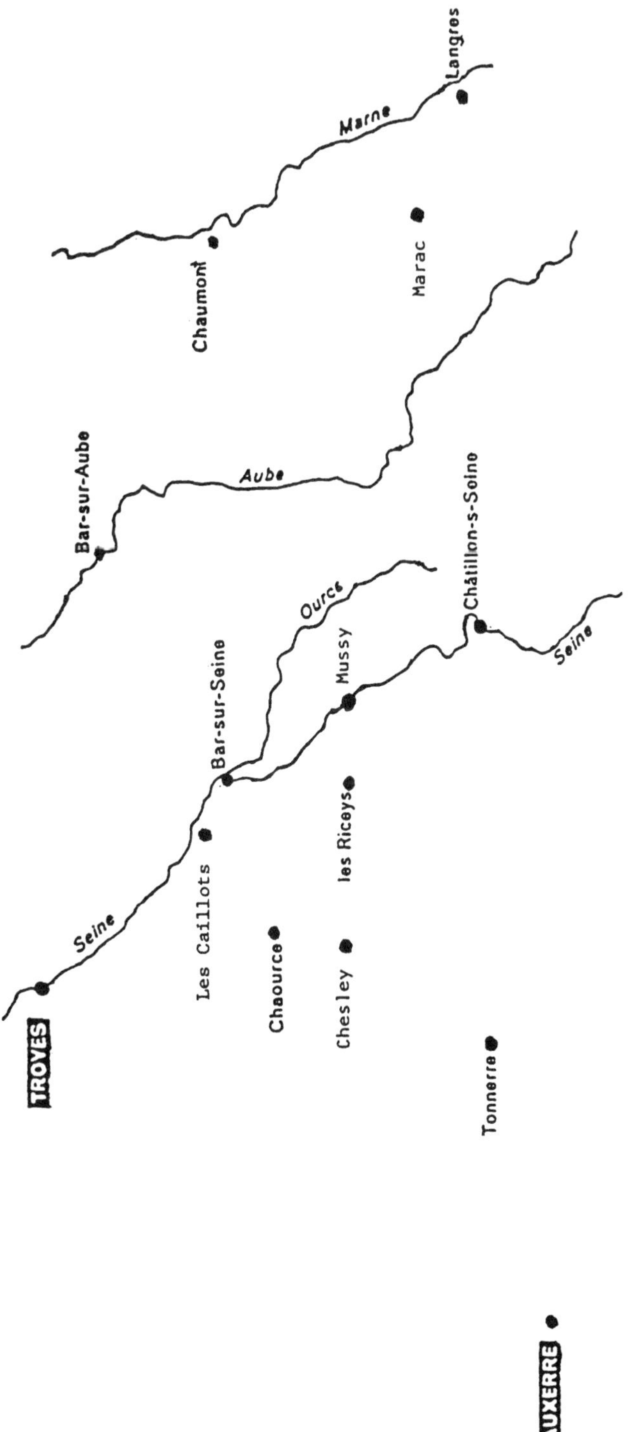

Fig. 1. Map of the borderlands of Champagne and Burgundy.

apply to cousin Jacques, author of a six-volume chronicle of the diocese of Langres (now Paris, Bibl. nat. France, MS fr. 5993-5998), in which appears his fable of the foundation of Mussy.[6] His manuscript account of the fabled foundation reached a wider audience through its publication by Nicolas de La Brosse in *Description de la terre et baronnie de Ricey* (1654). Lambert, in 1878,[7] was the first to expose the fable of the foundation of Mussy by the crusader 'Gilles Vignier' and it is now universally dismissed for the fairy-tale it is.

But in exposing the mythical Gilles Vignier, Lambert substituted his own theory of the founder, one which—because it is associated with an indubitable historical individual—remains still current. Lambert suggested that the patron of the rebuilding and glazing of Mussy might be Guillaume de Mussy, *chevalier du roi* (d. 12 December 1306, 1307 or 1308). Guillaume was one of the crew of frequently unscrupulous functionaries surrounding Philippe le Bel, among them Enguerrand de Marigny and the notorious Nogaret. The historian Robert-Henri Bautier has traced his career and outlined his methods of extortion in a definitive biography.[8] He began his ascent as bailiff to the count of Champagne and then to the king; in mid-career, late in 1292, he was summarily disgraced and condemned by Parlement to repay the crown the enormous sum of 3,000 *livres tournois*; yet six years later (29 August 1298) he was back in grace, promoted as royal *enquêteur* and finally *pannetier du roi.* 'This high-ranking civil servant, having acquired most frequently by odious procedures a very solid fortune in land, ambitious, grasping and dishonest,'[9] seems an unlikely—and unquestionably unattractive—patron for the collegiate parish church of Mussy.

Bautier maintains that during Guillaume's years of disgrace he retired to Mussy, where he held land, funding at that time the new church and its decoration. While the hypothesis has won general acceptance, it seems to me highly questionable. First of all, was Guillaume really living in

[6] See Appendix I pp. 113-19 below. The fable of the foundation of Mussy appears in Paris, BNF fr. 5994 fols. 270v, 272r.

[7] Charles-Auguste-Joseph Lambert, *Histoire de la ville de Mussy-l'Evêque (Aube)* (Chaumont: 1878) pp. 350-55. See also Charles-Ludovic Ray, *Le Père Jacques Vignier, généalogiste de sa lignée* (Troyes: 1921) pp. 7-22.

[8] Robert-Henri Bautier, "Guillaume de Mussy, bailli, enquêteur royal, pannetier de France sous Philippe le Bel," *Bibliothèque de l'Ecole des chartes* CV (1944) pp. 64-98 (reprinted in Bautier, *Etudes sur la France capétienne: De Louis VI aux fils de Philippe le Bel*, Variorum CS 359 [Aldershot, Hants: 1992]).

[9] Paraphrased from Salet, "Mussy" p. 330.

Mussy during his disgrace ca. 1293-98? The two documents cited by Bautier are known only from Vignier's chronicle.[10] And since Guillaume was then off the payroll—and the 3,000 *livres* had been paid for him by a Templar—it seems unlikely that he was then in a financial position for such theorized largesse. More basic is the question of whether Mussy really dates in the years just preceding 1300.

Furthermore, the identification of Guillaume de Mussy as founder is based upon the connection to him of heraldry in the glass and elsewhere in the church, as will be explored below. This study will seek to overturn this identification, attempt to correct it, and ultimately to propose a new and precise dating, major patron and a *raison d'être* for the glazing of Mussy-sur-Seine. The guiding patron was, I submit, not a corrupt man but a virtuous woman: Marguerite de Bourgogne (d. 1308), countess of Tonnerre and widowed queen of Jerusalem, Naples and Sicily through her marriage with the Capetian prince Charles d'Anjou, brother of St Louis, and in her retirement the revered benefactress of the remarkable medieval hospital that survives at Tonnerre.

Not a Corrupt Man...

A coat of arms in the stained glass of Mussy-sur-Seine (Fig. 28), now commonly identified with Guillaume de Mussy, displays *de gueules au chef d'argent à la bande componée d'argent et de sable brochant sur le tout, à la bordure d'azur.* This shield is now located in Bay 101 (see Fig. 2), placed in the current arrangement by the restorer Edouard-Amédée Didron ca. 1892-97.

Didron's restoration could be characterized as a 'tidying up,' an approach typical of the late nineteenth century. What had confronted him at Mussy had been a chaotic hodgepodge of glass panels and fragments herded without formal or logical sequence into a collage filling the three central bays of the apse (see Figs. 4, 5), clearly the result of the type of previous restoration one might designate a 'roundup' or 'consolidation of assets' approach.[11] The roundup (installing together surviving fragments from disparate locations) was most current in the era when stained glass no longer was practiced as an art, that is, from the late seventeenth century until around 1840—by which time the generation

[10] Bautier p. 77, citing documents of 1296 and 1297 provided by Vignier (BNF fr. 5995 fol. 196v); p. 75, for the Templar who paid the 3,000 *livres.*

[11] Lambert pp. 370-71 mentions some of the interpolated panels and subjects at Mussy before Didron's restoration.

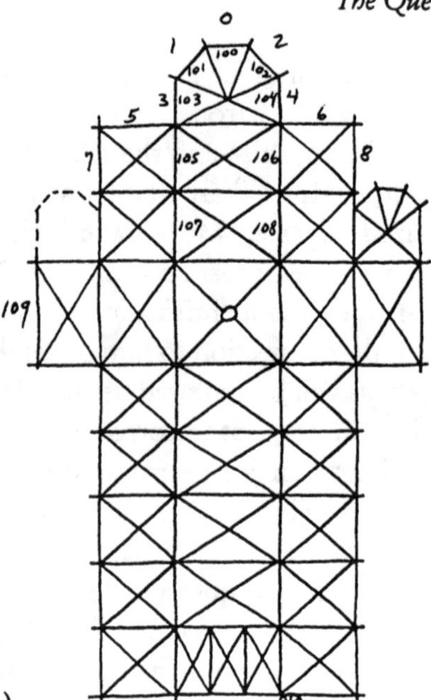

Fig. 2. Mussy-sur-Seine (Aube), Saint-Pierre-ès-Liens. Plan with bay numbers of windows. Ca. 1288-93. (Adapted from Branner)

born with no personal memory of the Revolution came to adulthood in France and began to debate what to do about its disintegrating patrimony. A very late example of a roundup restoration, at Evron (Mayenne) in 1839-40, was explained by the priest in charge of the operation: 'We had to collect the colored glass scattered here and there in the building, to compose complete bays of the five terminal windows of the apse.'[12] Since no restoration occurred at Mussy in the century between the Revolution and Didron, Mussy's roundup presumably had taken place about 1741, year of the major structural campaign by the bishop of Langres to save and restore the choir that was under his jurisdiction.[13]

An old photo shows the presumed 'Guillaume de Mussy escutcheon' at the bottom center of Bay 101 (Fig. 4) and Charles Fichot's watercolor of 1840 (Arch. dépt. Aube 5 Fi 4, fol. 137) confirms that it was then

[12] Abbé Gérault's account of his restoration of Evron is reprinted and discussed in Lillich, *The Armor of Light, Stained Glass in Western France 1250-1325* (Berkeley: 1994) p. 264. Earlier examples are restorations at Sainte-Radegonde, Poitiers, designated by me as the 'patchwork of scraps' (?17th c.) and the 'consolidation of assets' (1708): *Armor* pp. 79-81.

[13] Edouard de Barthélemy, ed., *Voyage littéraire de Dom Guyton en Champagne (1744-1749)* (Paris: 1889) p. 174: the Cistercian Dom Guyton visited Mussy in 1744, after the choir had been repaired. Anne Pinto discusses documents on pp. 16-17 of her thesis (as in n. 1 above) concerning the bishop's restoration of the choir as well as the nave, responsibility of the town, finally restored by 1756 (Arch. dépt. Haute-Marne G752 no. 20, G753 no. 44).

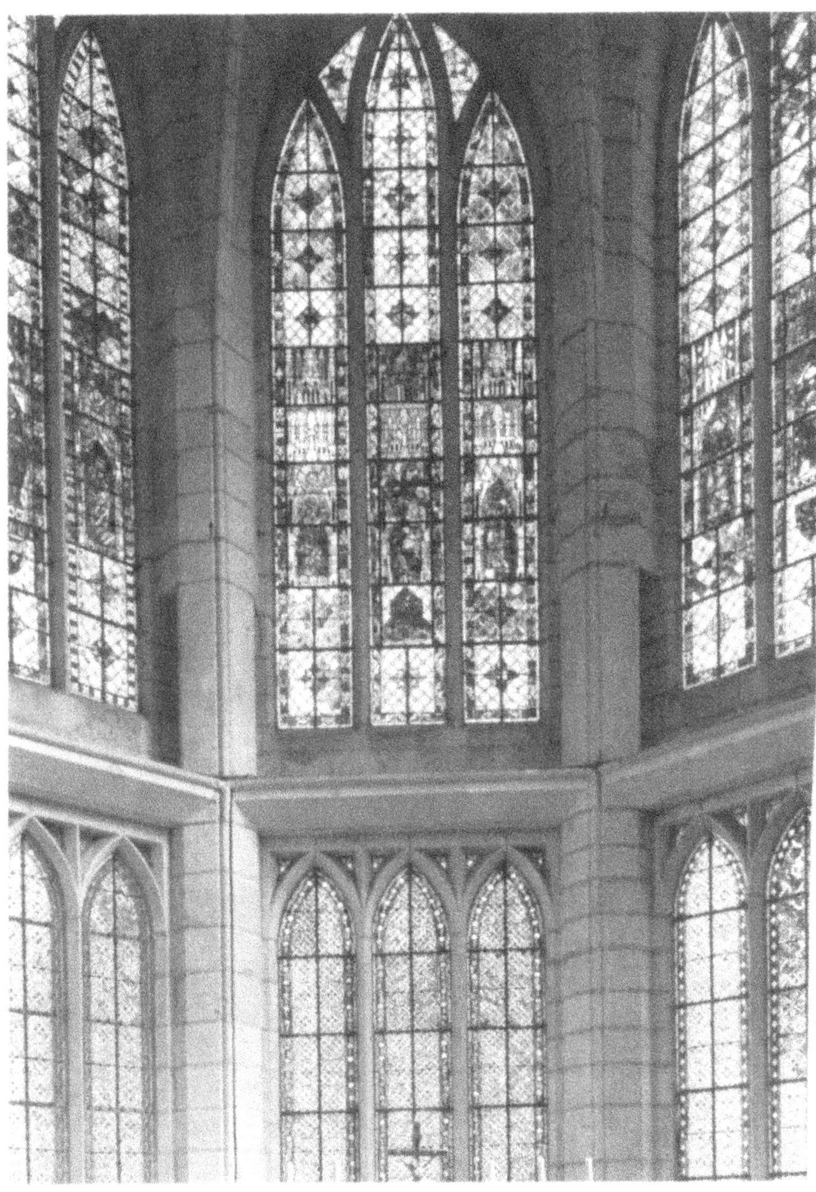

Fig. 3. Mussy. Bays 101, 100, 102 and 1, 0, 2 (left to right). Ca. 1288-93. (Photo: E. Millet, Inventaire général 1988)

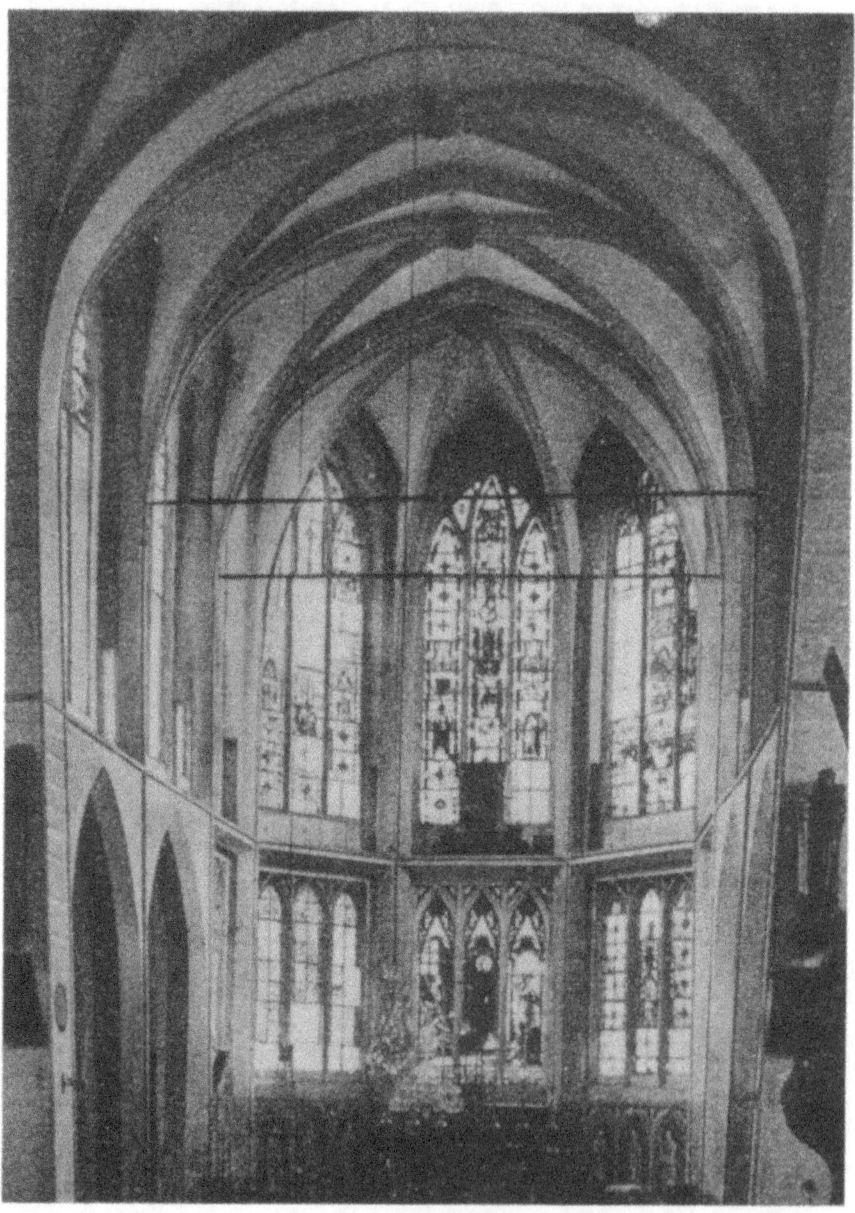

Fig. 4. Mussy. Interior of choir, October 1884. Bays 101, 100, 102 and 1,0,2. (Photo: E. Durand, Paris, Arch. phot. no. 6589; after Schürenberg 1934)

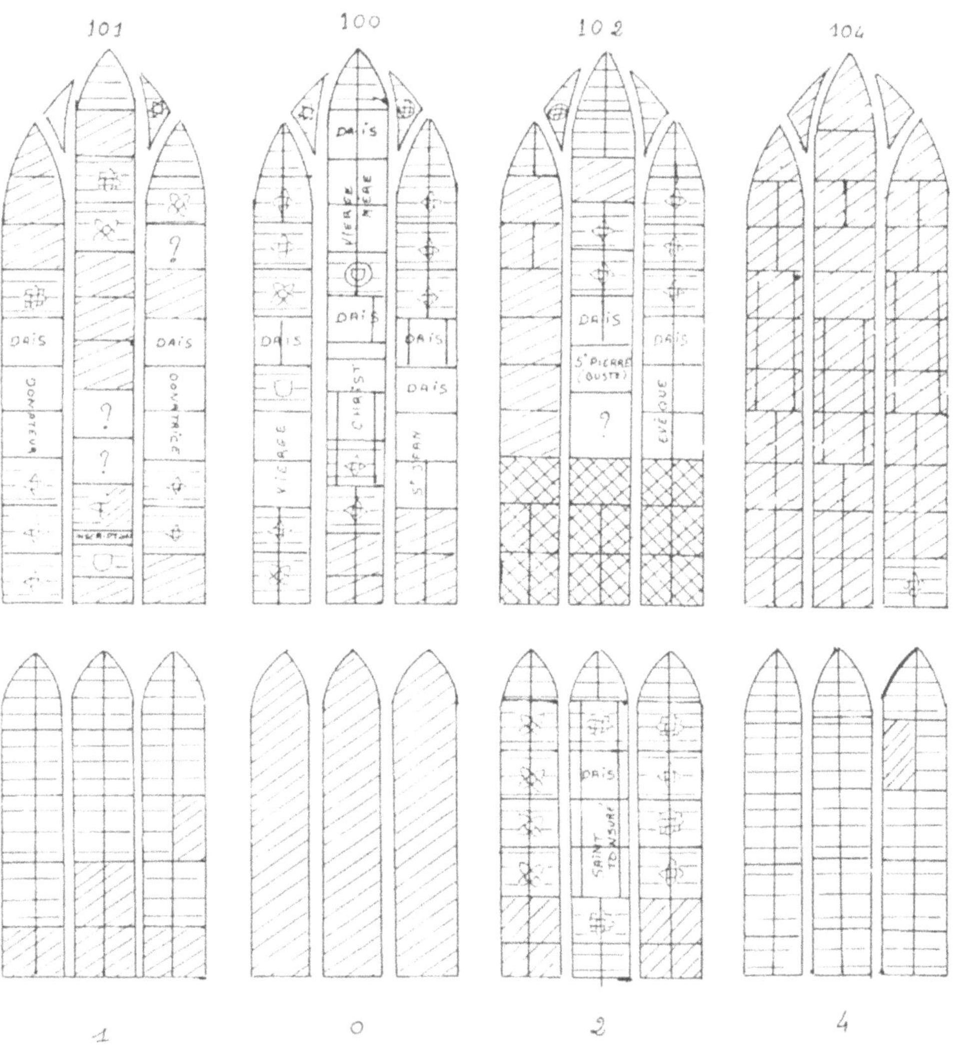

Fig. 5. Mussy. Stained glass before 1884. Diagram by Anne Pinto, based on old photos; Bay 103 is omitted because no old photo exists.
Horizontal lines = grisaille
Diagonal lines = white modern glass
Crosshatched lines = Sixteenth-century glass (Adam & Eve)
? = unidentified figural subject

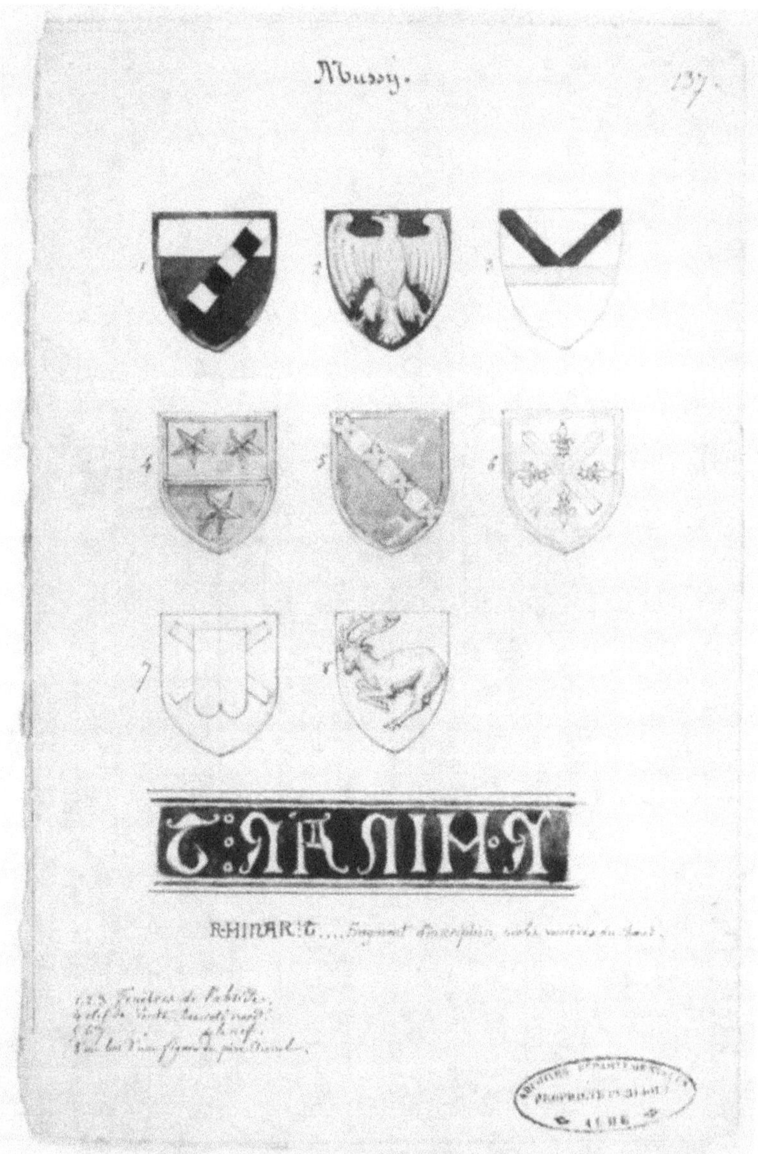

Fig. 6. Mussy. Coats of arms and inscription recorded by Charles Fichot, 1840 watercolor (Arch. dépt. Aube, 5 Fi 4, fol. 137). Identifications in p. 53 n. 73 below. (Photo: Arch. dépt. Aube)

1, 2, 3 = stained glass in apse
4 = keystone of north nave aisle
5, 6, 7 = keystones of nave vaults
8 = below God the Father (15th c. sculpture of the Trinity)
Inscription fragment = in Bay 101

installed backwards (paint-side out)[14] and thus had been moved there. (Cf. Fig. 6 no. 1 and Fig. 28) While the original location of this shield is unrecorded, Vignier (BNF fr. 5994 fol. 270v) and de La Brosse report in the choir windows a kneeling knight in heraldic surcoat of the same arms—a figure now lost.[15] In this instance they may be believed, since their observations could have been checked by any casual observer who cared to walk into the church around 1650.

It is a relatively simple matter to establish that this shield (and the lost image of the kneeling knight) cannot refer to Guillaume de Mussy. One of the surest proofs of medieval heraldry is found in seals, and Guillaume—both before (1282, 1283) and after (1299) his years of disgrace—sealed with the arms *d'azur au sautoir de gueules, cantonné de quatre fleurs de lis d'or.*[16] (See Fig. 7) The tinctures do not appear on his seals, of course, but can be easily supplied since these are the arms of the bishops of Langres, whose summer château was at Mussy, and who remained the only seigneur of the town from the mid-thirteenth century until the Revolution. The arms appear on their coins, seals, and perhaps one tomb. The tomb is problematical since it is mentioned only by Père Vignier. Two examples of the arms, he affirmed, were engraved on the tomb of Bishop Joceran de Brancion (d. 1126) in the church of Saint-

---

[14] Also visibly reversed in old photos were the two kneeling donors now in the flanking lancets of this bay. Fichot's unpublished drawings are listed in *Annuaire de l'Aube* (1904) p. 21; the Arch. dépt. Aube has a microfilm of them (2 Mi 245). Witnesses between Fichot and the 1892-95 restoration include Lucien Coutant, "Sceau du chapitre de l'église de Mussy," *Recueil des travaux de la Société de sphragistique de Paris* II (1852-53) p. 314, who states that the window with the 'de Mussy' coat of arms was late fifteenth century. Presumably he was referring to Renaissance panels grouped in the axial bays in the 1740 roundup restoration. Fichot's drawing of the coats of arms was verified in the church by Charles Nioré in the early 1890s: Troyes, Bibl. mun. MS 3089, v. III fol. 869r-v (notes on paper printed with the date 189_).

[15] The statements of Vignier and de La Brosse are quoted by Lambert pp. 351, 353; for de La Brosse see also Charles-Ludovic Ray, *Une Légende pour rire concernant les Riceys* (Arcis-sur-Aube: 1914) pp. 14-15.

[16] His seal of 1282 (37 mm.) survives on Arch. dépt. Marne 1 G 1466 and 17 H 132/11; the seal of 1283 (23 mm.) is on Arch. dépt. Marne 1G 1377; the seal of 1299 (small, size not available) is on Arch. dépt. Haute-Marne G474. The latter seal is included in the typed list, "Arch. Nat., Service des sceaux, Repertoire numérique des sceaux conservés dans les Arch. dépt. H M recensés par M. Auguste Coulon pour l'Inventaire des sceaux de Champagne" (1963). I have checked every charter of Guillaume de Mussy cited in Bautier's study; many of those listed as *scellé* no longer retain their seals. I would like to thank Marie-Josèphe Gut (Arch. dépt. Oise) and Catherine Marion (Arch. dépt. Marne) for their very generous responses to my written inquiries.

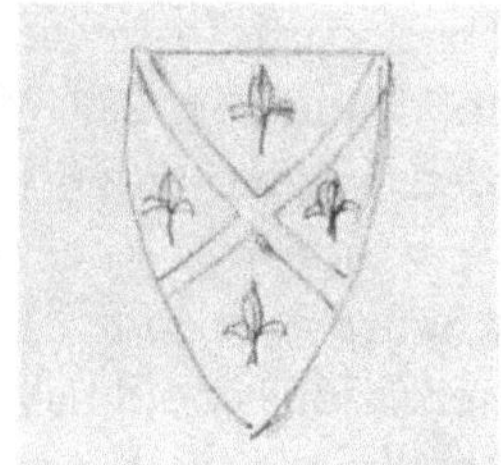

Fig. 7. Seal used by Guillaume de Mussy, 1282 (37 mm.; Arch. dépt. Marne, 1 G 1466 and 17 H 132/11). Arms are those of the bishopric of Langres, seigneur of Mussy-sur-Seine: *sautoir, cantonné de quatre fleurs de lis.* (Drawing: Catherine Marion)

Etienne, Dijon.[17] Whether or not one can trust Vignier concerning this early tomb, there is good numismatic and sigillographic evidence. The coinage of the bishops of Langres, in widespread usage in the middle ages, was changed to include the heraldic *sautoir cantonné de quatre fleurs de lis* most probably by Bishop Robert de Thorotte, who issued a charter in 1238 mentioning his wish to modify the coinage.[18] It seems to have been somewhat precocious in this regard, as heraldic coinage appeared in Burgundy only under Duke Robert II (1272-1305), in the county of Nevers after 1257, and in Brittany under Duke Jean I (1237-86). At any rate, such heraldic coins (Fig. 8) were issued in Langres by Bishops Gui de Rochefort (1250-66), Gui de Genève (1266-91) and Guillaume de Durfort (1306-19).[19] The earliest seal including the arms of the bishopric is dated 1317 (Guillaume de Durfort, Fig. 9).[20]

Thus Guillaume de Mussy used as his seal the arms of his seigneur;

---

[17] Lambert discusses the arms of the bishops of Langres pp. 342-48. On the tomb of Joceran de Brancion, caveat lector! See Arthur Daguin, "Les Evêques de Langres, étude épigraphique, sigillographique et héraldique," *Mémoires de la Société historique et archéologique de Langres* III (1880) p. 82, citing Vignier and the *Annuaire de la Haute-Marne* of 1808 by Abbé Jean-Baptiste-Joseph Mathieu (1764-1829), one of whose main sources was Vignier (reprinted as Mathieu, *Abrégé chronologique de l'histoire des évêques de Langres*, 2nd ed. [Langres: 1844] p. 63). The collection of tomb drawings made by Gaignières (d. 1715) does not include Joceran de Brancion's tomb, though it does have another from the same church: Jean Adhémar, "Les Tombeaux de la collection Gaignières," II, *Gazette des beaux-arts* CXVIII (6e période v. LXXXVIII) (1976) p. 17 no. 1174.

[18] The charter is published by Anatole de Barthélemy, "Une Monnaie inédite de Langres," *Bulletin de la Société historique et archéologique de Langres* I (1880) pp. 269-70.

[19] Emile Caron, *Monnaies féodales françaises* III (Paris: 1882-84) pp. 335-36. The coins of Guillaume de Durfort were previously attributed to Guillaume de Joinville (1209-19): Faustin Póey d'Avant, *Monnaies féodales de France* III (Paris: 1862) p. 223, pl. CXXXV nos. 14-16. See also: Philippe Salmon, "Notice sur plusieurs monnaies épiscopales inédites de Langres," *Revue de la numismatique belge* 2e série v. V (1855) pp. 29-30, pl. II no. 3; Pierre-Ancher Tobiesen Duby, *Traité des monnaies des barons...* I (Paris: 1790) p. 34, pl. X nos. 2-4.

[20] Louis Douët-d'Arcq, *Collection de sceaux* II (Paris: 1867, rpt. Munich: 1980) p. 509 (no. 6625).

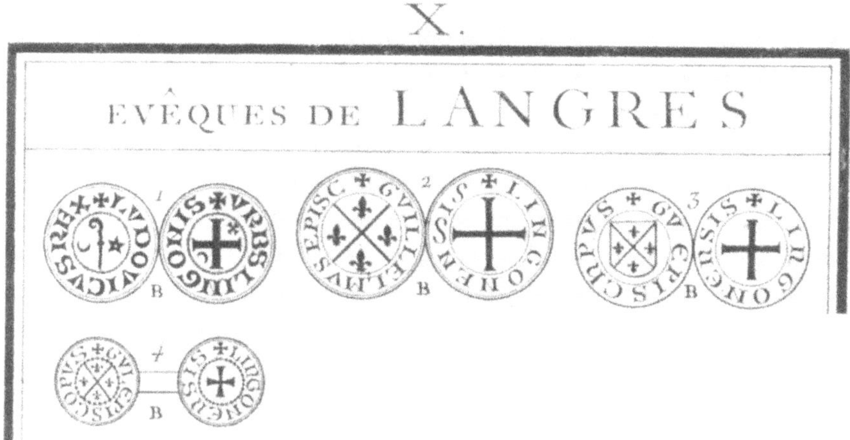

Fig. 8. Coins of bishops of Langres. Coat of arms on nos. 2-4, used by Gui de Rochefort, Gui de Genève, and Guillaume de Durfort: *sautoir, cantonné de quatre fleurs de lis.* (After Duby 1790) (Photo: Paris, Bibliothèque nationale de France)

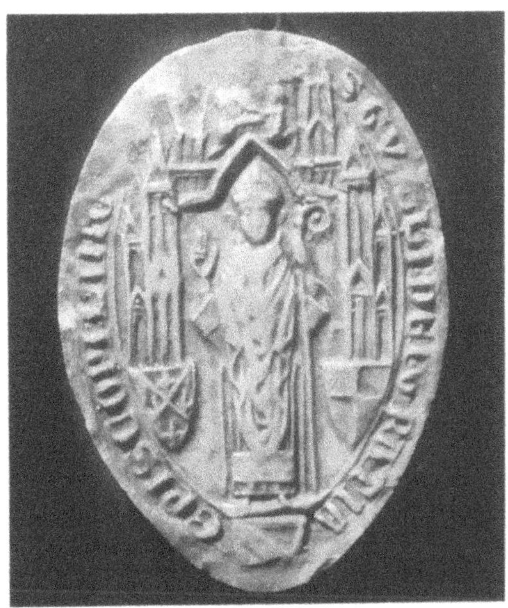

Fig. 9. Seal of Bishop Guillaume de Durfort, 1317, showing (right) his family arms and (left) arms of bishops of Langres: *sautoir, cantonné de quatre fleurs de lis.* Douët-d'Arcq 6625. (Photo: Archives nationales)

his grandfather Guiard Pignot (d. after 1244) had served the bishop as his *châtelain* of Mussy.[21] There is no evidence that Guillaume's family of "petite féodalité" had been armigerous, and Père Anselme (d. 1694), who discusses him in his section on the *pannetiers du roi*, gives no arms for him.[22]

It must be allowed that Guillaume contributed two houses "by the bridge" to the bishop in 1287, and further revenues in 1300 (thus both before and after his disgrace).[23] But he is neither the founder of the new church nor the donor of its stained glass.

The assumption that Guillaume de Mussy was the patron behind the new construction at Mussy was based on an incorrect dating of the church (to the period coinciding with his years of disgrace), and on the misinterpretation of one of its stained glass coats of arms (Fig. 28) as his. If he did not use those arms, the problem remains of who did. Before that question can be addressed, an investigation of the stylistic evidence may provide a more accurate dating of the glazing, and ultimately the probable moment when the new construction was undertaken.

---

[21] Michel Belotte, "Les Possessions des évêques de Langres dans la région de Mussy-sur-Seine et de Châtillon-sur-Seine du milieu du XIIe au milieu du XIVe siècle," *Annales de Bourgogne* XXXVII no. 147 (Jul-Sept 1965) p. 191; also Bautier pp. 66-67 and Lambert p. 176. A pamphlet guide for sale in the church ("Mussy-sur-Seine. Eglise Saint-Pierre," p. 6) states that Guillaume de Mussy began his career as provost (*viguier*) of Mussy, thus in the employ of the bishop and charged with maintenance of the town's fortifications. However, I have found no verification for these assertions.

[22] Père Anselme, *Histoire de la maison royale de France et des grands officiers de la couronne*, 3rd rev. ed. (1726-33, rpt. 1967) VIII p. 607. On Guillaume de Mussy's ancestry see Bautier pp. 66-68.

[23] Lambert pp. 174-75, 355, and text of charter pp. 537-38; Belotte p. 190; Bautier p. 72. On Guillaume's gift of 1287 see below p. 63 n. 98.

PART II

MUSSY: WHAT ORNAMENT AND HERALDRY REVEAL

One often learns a great deal from careful study of ornament, such as borders and grisaille. Mussy presents a fascinating assortment of both. To begin with the most puzzling, two unrelated genres of grisaille are curiously juxtaposed: the clerestory grisailles are a fairly standard type for the late thirteenth century, while the lower windows of the apse contain a much rarer type of unpainted grisaille known as blank-glazing and commonly associated with early Cistercian churches (Figs. 3, 10). The term blankglazing derives from the patterns that are formed without painting, by the leads alone. The five lower bays were 'tidied up' by Didron between 1888 and 1890, but older photos indicate that the axial bay had been blinded (to increase stability?) and Bay 2 invaded by alien fragments,[1] no doubt in the 'roundup' restoration ca. 1740.Three blank-glazing patterns now remain, and a fourth is preserved not only in Fichot's 1840 drawing but in a drawing by Ottin as well, first published in 1896 (Fig. 11 nos. 1-4 and Fig. 12).[2]

Blankglazing occurs in early Cistercian churches from the earliest survivals until about 1250. Examples remain in France, Germany, and (recently published) at Santes Creus in Catalonia.[3] The Cistercians employed two distinct types of blankglazing patterns, one group incorporating floral or vegetal motifs—apparently unique to Cistercian churches—and a second type of grisaille of geometric interlace patterns, which

---

[1] Lambert p. 370 mentions the blinded axial bay in the lower row of windows. In the nineteenth century Bay 2 contained the standing deacon under canopy, flanked by grisailles of the clerestory type (see my Fig. 4); Didron moved these panels into Bay 102.

[2] On Fichot's drawings see p. 11 n. 14 above. Ottin's drawing: Léon-Auguste Ottin, *Le Vitrail* (Paris: 1896) p. 35 fig. 33 (and several later editions). Ottin was a glass painter active from 1861-90. Since this fourth pattern was eliminated from the blankglazing restored to the church in 1890, he must have seen it in Didron's studio.

[3] Helen Zakin, *French Cistercian Grisaille Glass* (New York: 1979); see also Lillich, "Recent Scholarship Concerning Cistercian Windows," in *Studiosorum Speculum: Studies in Honor of Louis J. Lekai, O.Cist.*, ed. Francis Swietek and John Sommerfeldt (Kalamazoo: 1993) pp. 233-62, which is the basis for the following paragraph.

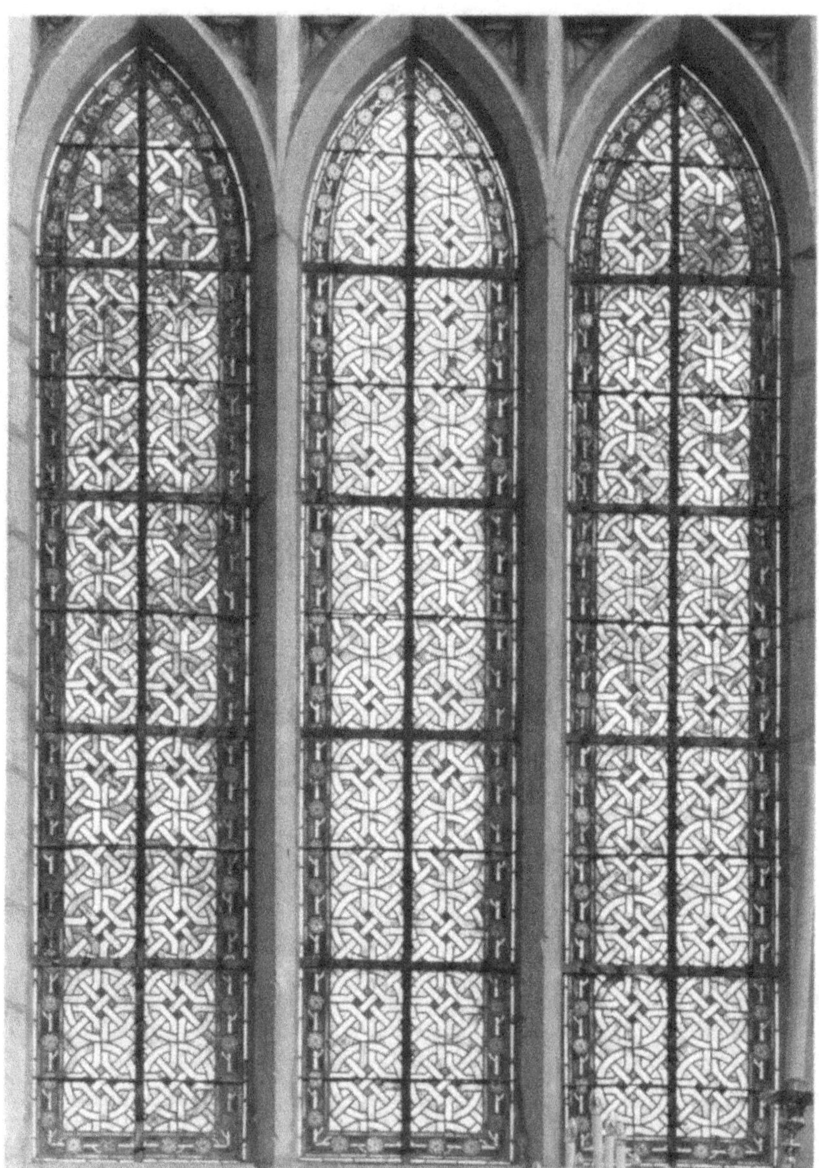

Fig. 10. Mussy. Bay 1. Grisaille blankglazing; border is made of marguerites of the queen of Sicily, ca. 1288-93. (Photo: E. Millet, Inventaire général 1988).

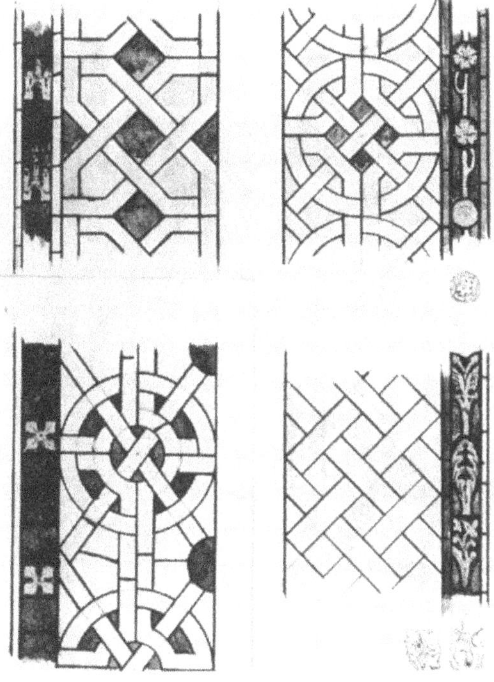

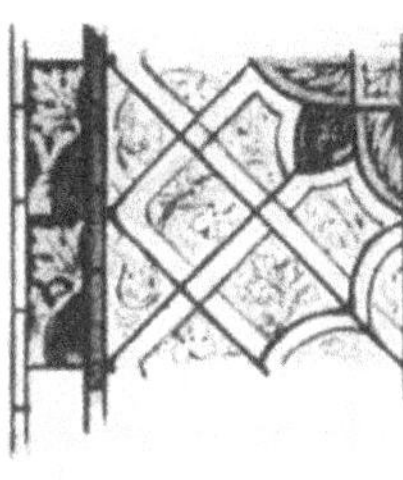

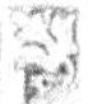

Fig. 11. Mussy. Grisailles recorded by Charles Fichot, 1840 watercolor (Arch. dépt. Aube, 5 Fi 4, fol. 129 and 129bis). (Photo: Arch. dépt. Aube). Blankglazing = nos. 1-4; clerestory grisaille = no. 5.

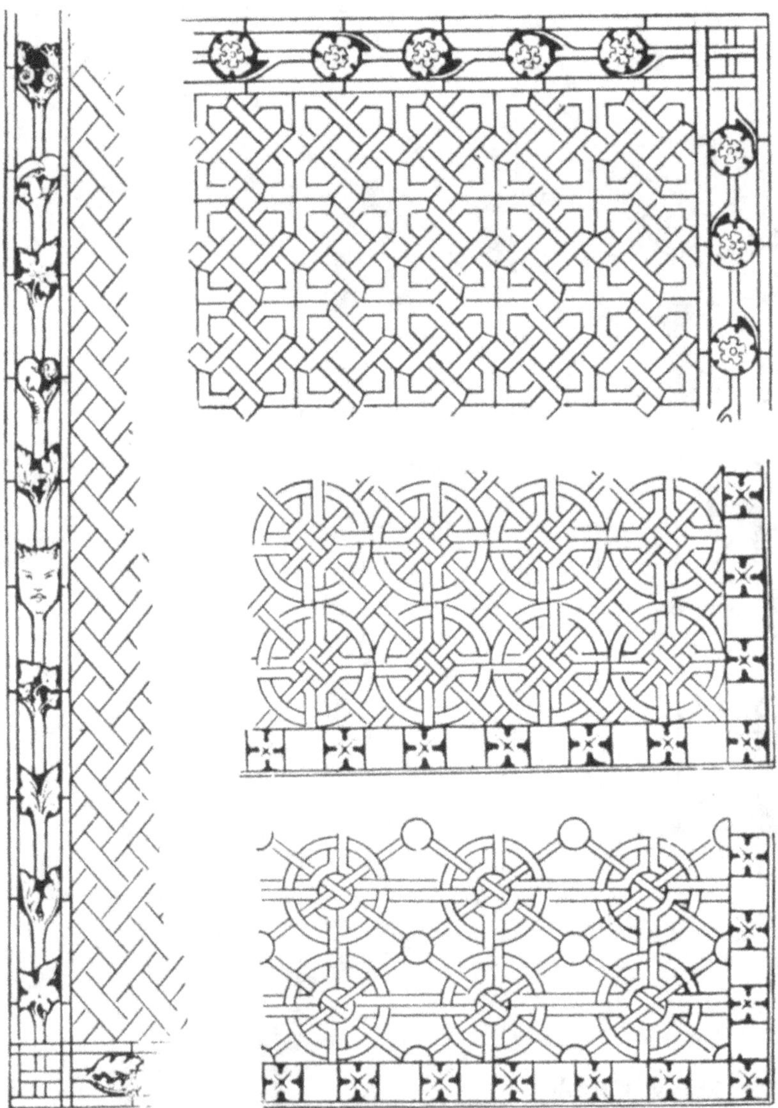

Fig. 12. Mussy. Grisaille blankglazing (after Ottin, 1896).

they seem to have adapted to their meditative purposes from general glazing practice in their 'home counties' of Champagne and Burgundy.

The Benedictine abbey of Orbais (Marne) preserves four patterns of geometric blankglazing amidst a great abundance of decorative window types. Françoise Gatouillat, profiting from work on the census of Burgundian windows for the French Corpus Vitrearum, has provided data on examples no longer extant from the parish church of Migennes, the collegiate churches of Montréal and Saint-Martin de Chablis, and the Hôtel-Dieu of Sens. More exciting are her two surviving examples, in the small church of Cudot (Yonne) and in an upper tower window in the façade of Sens cathedral.[4] None of these sites date later than the mid-thirteenth century, by which time geometric blankglazing appears to have gone out of fashion for Cistercians and non-Cistercians alike. A little-known later example, however, is the series of grisailles in the clerestory of Beauvais cathedral (ca. 1268-72).[5] A form of blankglazing typical of the Rhineland could also be mentioned, a viable tradition including several Alsatian examples of the last quarter of the thirteenth century, and at Toul in Lorraine in the fourteenth. But the Rhenish form remains limited to a simplified intersecting latticework, known in French as *à bâtons rompus*. Only one of Mussy's four patterns is *à bâtons rompus* (Fig. 11 no. 4, Fig. 12 left), and the pattern also occurs amid more complex designs at the earlier Burgundian sites listed above (as well as at Beauvais).

Thus Mussy seems to represent a vestige of the earlier traditions of its own region. Pinto has suggested the possibility of a reuse, since the glass is more greenish than in the clerestory grisailles above.[6] Since the church at Mussy replaces an earlier one, it is possible; the canons were

---

[4] Françoise Gatouillat, "Vitreries de type cistercien dans l'Yonne," in *Archéologie, histoire et folklore du nord de l'Yonne*, Actes du 56e Congrès de l'Association bourguignonne des sociétés savantes (Villeneuve-sur-Yonne: 1985) pp. 59-64; see also *Les Vitraux de Bourgogne, Franche-Comté et Rhône-Alpes*, Corpus Vitrearum France, Recensement III (Paris: 1986) pp. 138-39, 204.

[5] Michael Cothren, "The Thirteenth- and Fourteenth-Century Glazing in the Choir of the Cathedral of Beauvais," Ph.D. dissertation, Columbia 1980, pp. 172-74, pls. 103, 105, 110, 111, 115 (left).

[6] Pinto thesis (as in p. 1 n. 1 above) pp. 63-64. She notes the proximity of Pontigny and Fontenay; nearby Pothières was, however, Benedictine (see below p. 73 at nn. 9-10). The closest Cistercian abbey was Mores (founded 1153 from Clairvaux), the lands of which adjoined Mussy to the north. On Mores see: L.-H. Cottineau, *Répertoire topobibliographique des abbayes et prieurés* II (Mâcon: 1935) col. 1982; Alphonse Roserot, *Dictionnaire historique de la Champagne méridionale (Aube) des origines à 1790* II (Langres: 1942, rpt. Marseille: 1983-84) pp. 970-73.

installed in the parish church in 1218. If that was the case the present lancet openings would have been designed expressly to accommodate the spolia from the replaced parish church within new borders. I will seek clues to the dating of the rebuilding campaign in those borders in the discussion below.

The Grisailles of the Clerestory

But first, the grisailles in the clerestories may also provide evidence for dating. The several patterns of painted grisaille at Mussy are of the standard late thirteenth-century type known as bulged quarries (Figs. 3, 22), that is, a repeated panel design in which a more or less regular latticework of filets bulges out of alignment around a central colored boss (and also, normally, around corner accents in each panel, though not in the Mussy design). Fichot's drawing (Fig. 11 no. 5) records the basic pattern, though his central *bosse* is a variant that no longer survives in the ensemble. Versions of the basic pattern occur with foliage resembling clover, ivy and maple, and with several minor alterations of the central motif. Although not a great many medieval grisaille panels have survived the centuries at Mussy (most of them now being Didron's copies), two variants from the basic pattern do appear, evidence that grisaille as well as colored glass was herded into the apse ca. 1740—and that the original glazing ensemble must have been quite homogeneous. For the two variants are extremely close to the basic pattern. One (now in Bay 100, the upper panels of the flanking lancets, Fig. 3) varies only in presenting a completely straight, unbulged latticework of filets; the other (several panels in the upper right lancet of Bay 101) presents the basic pattern but with more feathery geranium-type leaves against an old-fashioned cross-hatched ground. All other grounds at Mussy are clear and unpainted, as is standard by 1290.[7]

Such bulged quarries appear in the 1260s, along with such new elements as naturalistic foliage growing upward from a central stem and occasional clear, unhatched grounds.[8] The generation from 1260/95

[7] The nave clerestory grisailles at Saint-Père de Chartres, ca. 1306-15, are the exceptions that prove this rule. Presumably their cross-hatched grounds were intended to harmonize with the much earlier grisailles re-used in the straight choir bays.

[8] I have discussed the development of grisaille in a number of venues: Lillich, "A Redating of the Thirteenth-Century Grisaille Windows of Chartres Cathedral," *Gesta* XI/1 (1972) pp. 11-18; Lillich, "Three Essays on French Thirteenth Century Grisaille Glass," *Journal of Glass Studies* XV (1973) pp. 69-78. A general comparison to Mussy can be made at Dol

combines these new elements with the old in a bewildering range of designs. The appearance of all the new elements at Mussy, in close to a final definition, places the ensemble at the upper limit of that transitional period. By the fourteenth century the pattern normally straightens into an almost pure latticework of identical quarries and the foliage painting becomes much more nuanced and delicate. The leaves in the Mussy grisailles occasionally curl around the stem, which is not yet standard everywhere in the 1290s—it does not occur, for example, in the St Vincent chapel of Beauvais, dated 1290-95. The precocious appearance of curling leaves in the late grisailles of the Saint-Urbain de Troyes chapels (ca. 1285) suggests that eastern France was more advanced in this regard.[9]

An even more compelling regional comparison presents itself, to the somewhat more elegantly designed grisailles of the Hôtel-Dieu at Tonnerre, firmly dated to 1293-95 (Figs. 39, 49).[10] Mussy and Tonnerre both contain quasi-naturalistic foliage painted with a simple, forceful, direct touch, in a *panneautage* organized around the vertical axis. They share several idiosyncracies: there are no accents (or bulged filets) at all in the corners, as was more normally the case; and the filet pattern in both ensembles, as it hits the flanking borders, turns and aligns itself to run briefly along the border. A good contrast can be made with the ambulatory chapels of Evreux ca. 1295-1300, where standard bulged quarry patterns of naturalistic foliage on unpainted grounds have filets that 'bulge' around the corners of each panel and do not run in alignment with the vertical borders. The only real difference between Mussy and Tonnerre is that the glazier—for he must be the same—has produced a more sophisticated interlocking foliage pattern for the latter. He seems to be trying harder, and perhaps that is because he was working for a queen. To that remarkable woman homage will be paid shortly.

Canopy work

The canopies in the Mussy band windows (Figs. 3, 14, 18) can also be dated around 1290. The general development of crockets in the thirteenth century, from none at all to palmette crockets curled down, to more natural forms often turned frontally toward the viewer, to 'frayed cab-

---

cathedral ca. 1285f.: Lillich, *Armor* pp. 152-54.

[9] Beauvais: Cothren pl. 128. Saint-Urbain: Lillich, "Three Essays" p. 77.

[10] Pinto (thesis pp. 69-70) also came to this conclusion.

bage' leaves aimed upward, has reached the final development at Mussy. A good comparison can be made with the crockets lining the canopy gables in the straight choir windows of La Trinité at Vendôme, dated ca. 1285-90, where, as at Mussy, the gable over the figure is backed with a solid mass of double-line brickwork and fenestration patterns.[11] At Vendôme the canopies now have lost their upper panels, however. For an example of the greatly enlarged *épi* found in Mussy Bay 101, one could cite Merton College, Oxford (1289-1311). The towers and flying buttresses of the upper canopy panels at Mussy can be compared to slightly more elaborate designs in the Beauvais chapel window given by Raoul de Senlis (1290-95).[12]

The Clerestory Borders

The borders offer a typical array of motifs commonly found together by the late thirteenth century (Figs. 13-15, 18): vegetation sprouting from a rising or undulating stem; fleurs de lis and castles; and simple cassette motifs (at Mussy, a quatrefoil). The 'growing' foliage border has the longest history and seems to have held its place as most prestigious; indeed it serves at Mussy to flank the extraordinary crucified Christ in the axial light of the church (Fig. 13). The remaining motifs share an intertwined development. *France* (gold fleurs de lis on blue) and *Castille* (gold castles on red) are of course ultimately heraldic references associated with Louis IX (Figs. 13 left, 15). Pinoteau has established that the castles do not refer to his mother Blanche, who did not use them on her seals, but to the claim of the Capetians to the crown of Castile, offered to Louis VIII by one of the warring factions there.[13] Fleurs de lis and castles became a ubiquitous fashion in French glazing from about 1250 until the death of Philippe le Hardi in 1285. When the adolescent and traumatized Philippe le Bel unexpectedly came to the throne in that year he turned his back on Spain, and the castles lost any validity. The fashion, which of course had hardly anything at all to do with such political immediacies,

---

[11] On the development of canopy crockets see Lillich, *Armor* pp. 232-33. For Vendôme see pl. 50.

[12] Louis Grodecki and Catherine Brisac, *Le Vitrail gothique au XIIIe siècle* (Fribourg: 1984) pp. 265-66 and fig. 177 (Oxford), pp. 155-56 (Beauvais).

[13] I have remarked on *France/Castille* borders most recently in *Rainbow Like an Emerald: Stained Glass in Lorraine in the Thirteenth and Early Fourteenth Centuries* (University Park, Pa: 1991) p. 88.

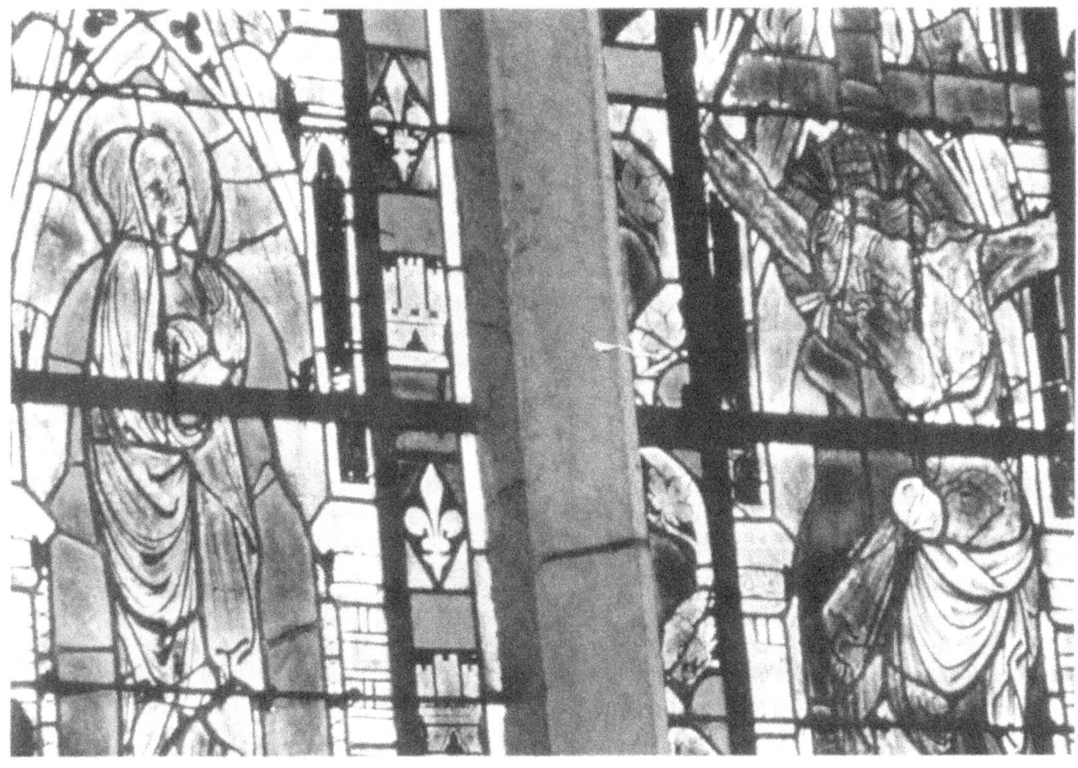

Fig. 13. Mussy. Bay 100. The Crucifixion. Ca. 1288-93. (Photo: Lillich).

hung on in stained glass for around five years, but after 1290 began to dissipate. Thereafter the castles (and sometimes fleurs de lis, too) appear in nonheraldic colors, or are replaced by simple, repetitive, abstract unit motifs (Fig. 14) which I have called 'cassettes.'[14] There are no fleurs de lis or castles in the Tonnerre borders of ca. 1295.

Thus the borders of Mussy can help in its dating, in spite of Didron's wholesale nineteenth-century replacements and the hodge-podge of stopgaps that had accumulated in the borders even before Didron's time.[15] The borders of alternating *France*[16] and *Castille* (in all three apsidal clerestories), juxtaposed with cassettes (Bay 101) and growing vegetation (100, 102) suggest a date for the upper windows no later than the late 1280s. A border of alternating *France* and *Castille* appears in the choir clerestory of Troyes in the 1240s, at Saint-Julien-du-Sault (Yonne) at the mid century, ca. 1255-60 at both Saint-Gengoult at Toul in Lorraine and at Gassicourt near Mantes west of Paris, and in the Vendôme hemicycle ca. 1280.[17] In most of these places it does seem to have carried some heraldic significance, at the least a political tilt toward France, at the most

[14] On borders ca. 1285 (at Dol) see Lillich, *Armor* pp. 152-53. For border patterns at Saint-Père see Lillich, *The Stained Glass of Saint-Père de Chartres* (Middletown, Conn.: 1978): in the 1290s, the hemicycle includes *France* alternating with cassettes as well as several designs with white fleurs de lis (pl. I frontispiece, pl. V); in the nave, dated 1306-15, there is a border of *Castille* alternating with cassettes (pl. IX) and a very odd one with white castles on gold (pl. VIII; also *Armor* pl. 59). But the final historiated bay of the church, Bay 18 (ca. 1315), reverts back to a border of pure *Castille*! (pls. XI, XII). Could this inexplicable border be a spolium from the campaign of 1260-70?

[15] The Mussy border that so fascinated Ottin (as in n. 2 above, p. 167; see my Fig. 12 left) is constructed of panels of two slightly different, alternating designs, and if indeed Ottin did not imagine the mushrooms, snails, etc., they must have been stopgaps of later glass. Fichot did not include them in his 1840 drawing of the same border (my Fig. 11 no. 4). As for Ottin's grimacing mask, Pinto's careful observation has located it in Bay 4, right border of the left lancet, at the top: Pinto p. 61 and pl. VII. It is unquestionably authentic. The doodle of an apprentice in the glazing shop, bored to death with the task of producing quantities of border foliage?

[16] Though Pinto (p. 71) did not find a single surviving medieval fleur de lis, one need not assume there were none. Arnaud and Aufauvre note their existence: Anne-François Arnaud, *Voyage archéologique et pittoresque dans le département de l'Aube* (Troyes: 1837) p. 224; Amédée Aufauvre, *Album pittoresque et monumental du département de l'Aube* (Troyes: 1852) p. 106. So does Lambert (1878, p. 371), who further states that the Conseil de la Commune ordered the fleurs de lis removed from the stained glass in 1793.

[17] See the discussion of *France/Castille* in Lillich, *Rainbow* pp. 36-37, pl. II.17; on Saint-Julien-du-Sault, see Virginia Raguin, *Stained Glass in Thirteenth-Century Burgundy* (Princeton: 1982) pls. 120, 120a; on Vendôme, Lillich, *Armor* pl. 48 (hemicycle windows given by Pierre d'Alençon, son of St Louis, discussed pp. 226-33).

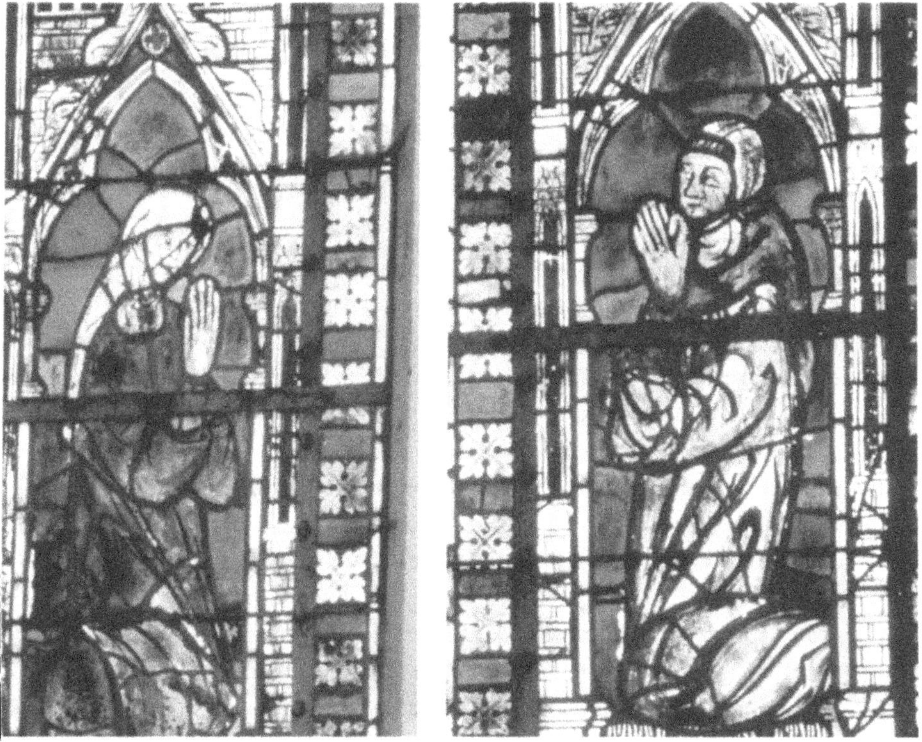

Fig. 14. Mussy. Bay 101. Lay donors, here identified as the mason Perrenet Barottier and his wife Jacquette. Ca. 1288-93. (Photo: Lillich).

a gift commissioned by a prince of the blood (at Vendôme).

In short, at Mussy I believe the apse clerestories were glazed as an integral part of the construction of the present church and funded (at least in part) by a patron or patrons who are thus revealed as politically affiliated with the Crown during the period ca. 1285-90. The powerful axial Crucifixion (Fig. 13) was clearly the core of this glazing program and the kneeling bishop now in Bay 102 matches its forceful style exactly (Figs. 15, 16). The bishop can be named: Gui de Genève, bishop of Langres (1266-died ca. Jan. 1291), whose strong royalist connections will be rehearsed below. Although the kneeling image is accompanied by no coat of arms, the vestments and crozier are glazed in Bishop Gui's heraldic colors, *azur* and *or*.[18] His seals also contain no explicit heraldic reference, and on both of his counterseals (Fig. 17)—unlike other bishops of Langres (Figs. 9, 27)—he is depicted kneeling.[19]

The Lower Borders and the Marguerites

The borders of the blankglazed grisailles include cassettes, white castles,[20] and in Bay 1 a most eccentric vegetation border composed of gold daisies (Figs. 10-12). The cassettes and the castles in non-heraldic white, as addressed above, appear around 1290. The unusual daisy border, moreover, reveals the donor. For this is the emblem of Marguerite de Bourgogne, queen of Sicily and countess of Tonnerre, widow of the Capetian prince Charles d'Anjou. Her movemented life and renowned charity will be reviewed below. She built the Hôtel-Dieu of Tonnerre from 1293 to 1295, as well as the adjoining château in which she then retired to finish her life in service to the poor and sick. The stained glass grisailles of Tonnerre, briefly mentioned above, contain as central bosses 'portrait busts' of Marguerite and her dead husband as well as shields with their heraldry (also in the floor tiles of her adjoining château), and one of the four border patterns of the Tonnerre glass (Figs. 37-39, 49A) recalls Mussy's daisies—which are marguerites.

The word 'marguerite' (from Latin *margarita*) originally meaning pearl, as in Matthew VII:6 ("pearls before swine"), was also used in this

[18] His arms were *d'azur à quatre points équipoles d'or* (reversed tinctures from the arms of his family, the counts of Genève). See Daguin, "Les Evêques de Langres" pp. 115-17.

[19] Auguste Coulon, *Inventaire des sceaux de la Bourgogne* (Paris: 1912) p. 164 nos. 956, 957.

[20] The white fleurs de lis in Bay 2 appear to be entirely Didron's.

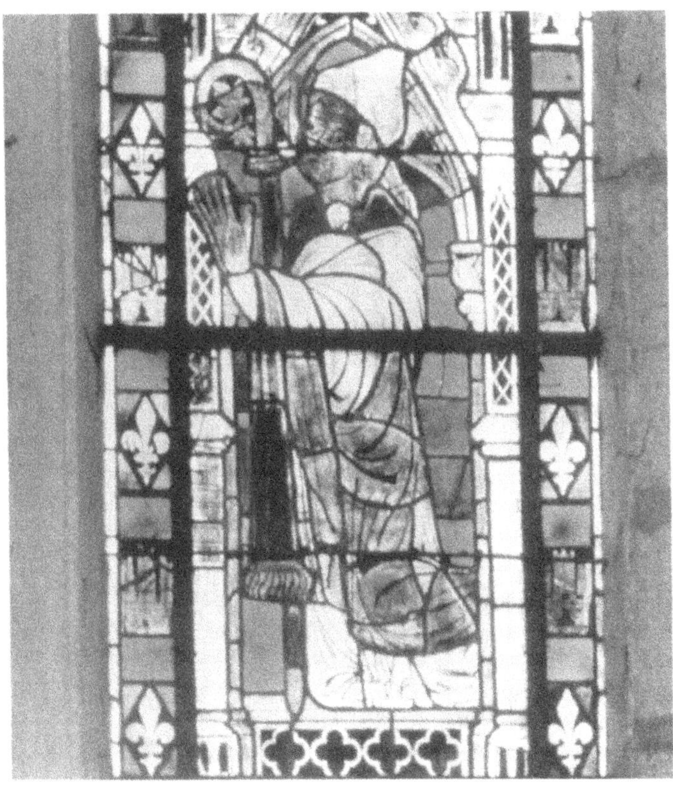

Fig. 15. Mussy. Bay 102. Bishop Gui de Genève. Ca. 1288-93. (Photo: Lillich)

Fig. 16. Mussy. Bay 102.
Bishop Gui de Genève, detail.
Ca. 1288-93.
(Photo: Jean Lafond).

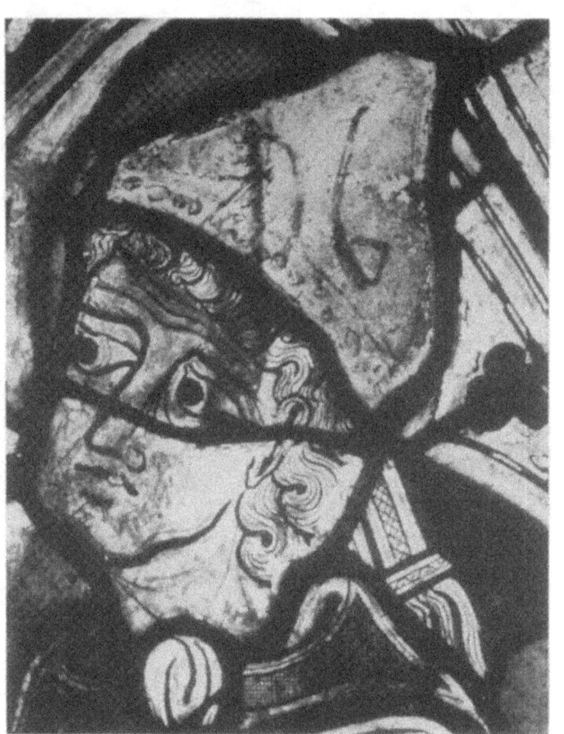

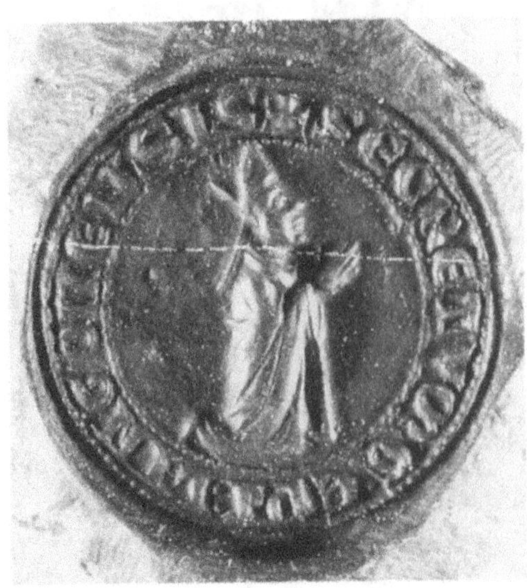

Fig. 17. Counterseal of Bishop Gui de Genève, 1275/76 (Arch. dépt. Côte-d'or, B1044, Coulon 957bis). (Photo: Arch. dépt. Côte- d'or).

sense by Wace and Rutebeuf. But marguerite clearly refers to a flower as used in *Aucassin et Nicolette* and by Guillaume de Machaut.[21] One might object that the Ox-Eye Daisy and Paris Daisy (bot. *Chrysanthemum leucanthemum* and *C. frutescens*) normally have white petals.[22] The Mussy border is composed of gold marguerites (on a red ground with a blue filet border) while those in the Tonnerre border are red with yellow stems on a blue ground. One might be excused for pointing out that red, blue and gold were the heraldic colors of Marguerite de Bourgogne as well as of her dead husband. Golden marguerites (*C. segetum*) have been known to botanists for some time, and an Anglo-Norman folk jingle specifically mentions red ones:[23]

> Marguerite,
> Fleur petite,
> Rouge au bord, verte autour,
> Dis le secret de mes amours.

The stained glass of Mussy does include white marguerites, prominently decorating the ground behind the standing deacon under canopy now in Bay 102 (Fig. 18), as well as the canopy panel now installed above the kneeling bishop in the same bay.[24] Equally compelling are the red marguerites—with white centers, a precocious instance of the glaziers' technique of engraving flashed ruby glass[25]—displayed in the ground of the deacon's canopy panel (Fig. 18, top). It is even possible that the large gold rosettes so conspicuously embellishing the three cano-

---

[21] *Trésor de la langue française, Dictionnaire de la langue du XIXe et du XXe siècle (1789-1960)*, XI, Centre nationale de la recherche scientifique (Paris: 1985) pp. 394-95; Emile Littré, *Dictionnaire de la langue française* III (Paris: 1875) p. 448.

[22] L. H. Bailey, *The Standard Cyclopedia of Horticulture* II (New York: 1914) pp. 756, 758.

[23] Edouard Le Héricher, *Histoire et glossaire du normand, de l'anglais et de la langue française* II (Paris: ca. 1862) p. 463; Littré p. 448.

[24] The canopy now over St Peter in the same bay is totally modern; in the nineteenth century Peter's head panel was in the central lancet. The original location of the canopy now over the bishop cannot be established. Old photos such as my Fig. 4 indicate that the deacon and his canopy were in Bay 2, no doubt moved there in the 1740 restoration.

[25] Pinto made this observation in her careful scrutiny of the Mussy windows (p. 90). She cites Mâle for an example of engraved ruby at Saint-Urbain de Troyes: Emile Mâle, "La Peinture sur verre de France," in André Michel, *Histoire de l'art depuis les premiers temps chrétiens jusqu'à nos jours* II, 1e partie (Paris: 1906) p. 393 n. 1. Earlier examples have recently been published from Strasbourg cathedral; for other thirteenth-century cases see Lillich, *Rainbow* p. 146 n. 106.

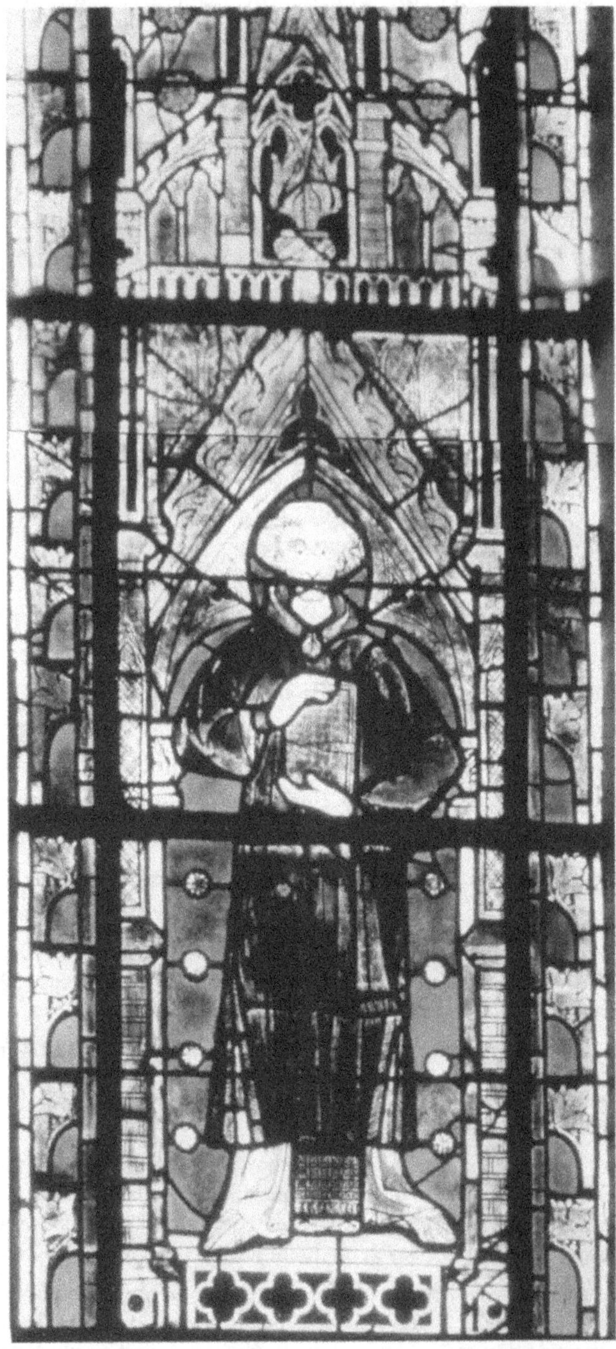

Fig. 18. Mussy. Bay 102. Tonsured deacon, here identified as St Vallier. Ca. 1288-93. (Photo: Lillich).

pies of the Crucifixion in Bay 100, just above the figures' heads, refer to Marguerite de Bourgogne as well.[26] The queen's underwriting of the Mussy glazing campaign appears to have been quite extensive and I will return to the question in the conclusion of this study. Indeed, only the glass now in Bay 101, the anonymous bourgeois couple who flank the Virgin, includes no marguerites of any kind.[27]

It might well be asked, since rosettes are so ubiquitous in Gothic arts of all media,[28] why they should be connected with Queen Marguerite in the instances of Mussy and Tonnerre. Certainly not all Gothic rosettes are name referents, though perhaps one should be more sensitive to the possibility of their serving as such signifiers. As early as 1234, the wedding ring given by Louis IX to his young bride Marguerite de Provence was formed of a garland of fleurs de lis and marguerite daisies.[29] A fourteenth-century example in eastern France is a tomb in Châlons cathedral depicting a mother and two daughters. The inscription of the mother (d. 1328) begins with a fleur de lis ('as if this mother was the queen of the family');[30] that of the elder daughter, d. 1313 probably in childbirth, begins with a cross; and that of the younger one, a nun d. 1338, commences with a five-petal rosette introducing the words "CI.GIST.MARGVERITE ...."

---

[26] The two rosettes in the flanking lancets, over the sorrowing Virgin and St John, are now modern, but part of the rosette over the Crucified Christ is original. See Recensement IV color pl. VIII opp. p. 141.

[27] Pinto p. 96 makes the reasonable suggestion that the couple originally flanked the Virgin now placed in Bay 104, who in the nineteenth century was in the top of the axial lancet of Bay 100. No marguerites decorate her either.

[28] An earlier example in glazing: Auxerre cathedral, the Magdalene and Mary of Egypt windows, illustrated in Raguin pls. 34, 35. Later examples: Troyes cathedral, nave chapels (bays 34, 51 in Recensement IV pp. 222, 226); Saint-Ouen de Rouen, axial chapel bay 42, illustrated in Jean Lafond, *Les Vitraux de l'église de Saint-Ouen de Rouen*, Corpus Vitrearum France IV-2/1 (Paris: 1970) pl. 5. Lafond (p. 30 n. 1) notes that the same border appears in the Rouen Lady chapel and in the Jumièges glass moved to La Mailleraye.

[29] Gérard Sivéry, *Marguerite de Provence* (Paris: 1987) p. 268 n. 36; Antoine-Pierre Lévis-Mirepoix, *Saint Louis, roi de France*, Le Mémorial des siècles—Les hommes (Paris: 1970) p. 64. Much later, in the 1360s-80s, the marguerite or French daisy became a common poetic motif and Guillaume Machaut even wrote a work entitled "Le dit de la Fleur de Lis et de la Marguerite:" see Peter Travis, "Chaucer's Heliotropes and the Poetics of Metaphor," *Speculum* LXXII/2 (April 1997) p. 403.

[30] Adolphe-Napoléon Didron, "Dalle funéraire de Châlons-sur-Marne," *Annales archéologiques* III (1846) pp. 282-90. The tomb is illustrated p. 282; the quote is p. 284; on p. 286 he interprets the five-petaled rosette as "une petite rose," though it is certainly a marguerite. The tomb is now upright in the south choir aisle.

So one might ask, are the rosettes on Marguerite de Bourgogne's seal of 1284, and on her counterseal (Fig. 19), meaningful or merely ornamental?[31] The evidence in the handsome floor tiles saved from Queen Marguerite's château at Tonnerre, however, is undeniable even to skeptics and has long been acknowledged. (See Figs. 20, 21). During the mid nineteenth-century demolition of the queen's residence adjoining the north flank of the hospital, tiles were discovered, then published by Amé, who commented on their heraldry:[32]

> Il est inutile de faire remarquer l'union intime qui existe entre les 'marguerites' et les 'fleurs de lys'. Ces emblèmes sont répétés sur chaque carreau: si l'un d'eux représente les armes de Bourgogne, une fleur de lys les surmonte; il en est de même si les armoiries d'Anjou y sont rendues, une marguerite les couronne....Ces armes d'Anjou et de Bourgogne, ces fleurs de lys et ces marguerites, mille fois répétées, ne sont-elles pas, pour ceux qui savent les comprendre, l'expression de l'amour, des regrets et du souvenir puissant que Marguerite conservait pour son époux.

---

[31] Seal of 1284, beneath her feet; counterseal, sexfoil frame. On her seals see Louis Le Maistre, "Sur les sceaux de Marguerite de Bourgogne, comtesse de Tonnerre, reine de Naples, de Sicile et de Jérusalem," *Recueil des travaux de la Société de sphragistique de Paris* II (1852-53) pp. 143, 148.

[32] Emile Amé, *Les Carrelages émaillés du moyen-âge et de la Renaissance* (Paris: 1859) Part II pp. 33-38, "Ancien château de Marguerite de Bourgogne." Surviving tiles from the château in regional museums: Matthieu Pinette, ed., *Les Carreaux de pavage dans la Bourgogne médiévale*, Musée Rolin (Autun: 1981) pp. 12, 44-45, nos. 264-70. On the tilehouse that produced them, some 15 km. distant at Villiers-Vineux: Jean-Paul Jacob and Henri Leredde, "La Terre cuite médiévale à Jaulges et Villiers-Vineux (Yonne). Point de la question," *Archéologie médiévale* VIII (1978) pp. 245-58. Identical tiles have been excavated from the site of the so-called 'Château du Roy' at Saint-Seine-sur-Vingeanne, which was a château of the Burgundian dukes from 1252-1477, probably destroyed 1513. Other heraldic motifs appear at Saint-Seine as well, and nothing would be *less* likely than that they would be "purement décoratifs et ne se rapportent à aucune famille déterminée" (Pinette p. 37). For drawings see Pinette (nos. 91-104) and M. Amiot and P. Radiet, "Les Carreaux vernissés du Château du Roy à Saint-Seine-sur-Vingeanne," *Mémoires de la Commission des antiquités du département de la Côte-d'Or* XXV (1959-62) pp. 234-41. Their attempt (pp. 240-41) to relate the heraldry to lower nobility of the immediate area is misguided. Without working up Saint-Seine for this footnote—which without tinctures would require some care—I would suggest the following families close to the Burgundian court: *dauphin* (Forez or Dauphins du Viennois); *lion couronné* (Grancey or Champlitte/Pontailler); *deux bars adossés* (Bar or Montbéliard); *bande* (undoubtedly Chalon, married to Queen Marguerite's sister); *alérion* (Antigny/Vienne); *clef en pal* (Thil-Châtel or Montjoie); *trois quintefeuilles* (de Vergy, Queen Marguerite's great-grandmother); *aigle* (Vienne or Joigny). For capsule histories of most of these families see Max Prinet, "L'Armorial de Bourgogne du Héraut Berry," *Le Moyen âge* 3e série v. II (1931) pp. 161-219.

(It is unnecessary to note the intimate union that exists between the marguerites and the fleurs de lis. These emblems are repeated on each tile: if a tile represents the arms of Burgundy, a fleur de lis surmounts them; it is the same if the arms of Anjou are depicted, they are crowned by a marguerite....These arms of Anjou and of Burgundy, these fleurs de lis and these marguerites, repeated a thousand times over, are they not, for those who know how to understand them, the expression of the love, regrets and powerful memory that Marguerite felt for her husband.)

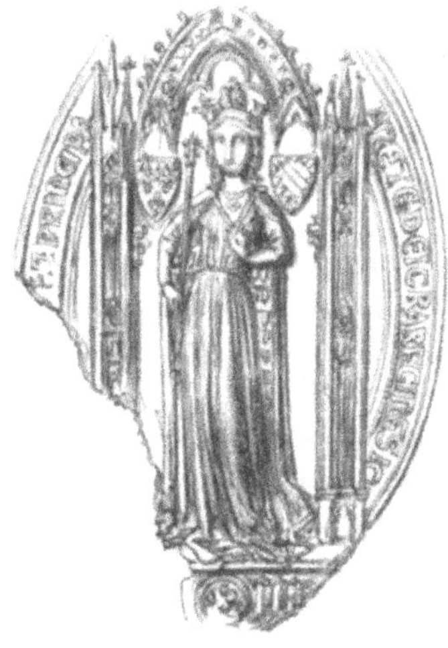

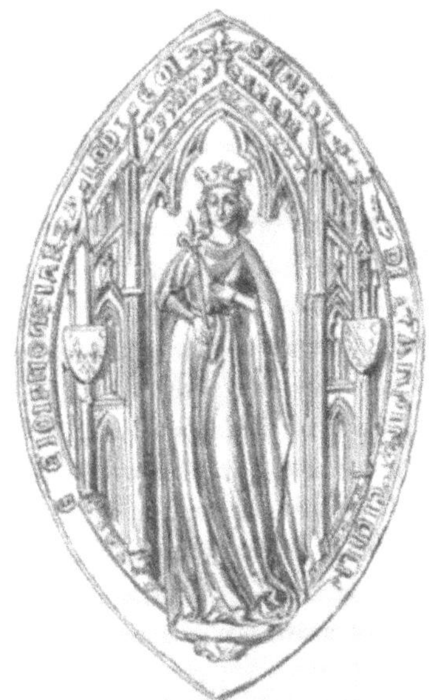

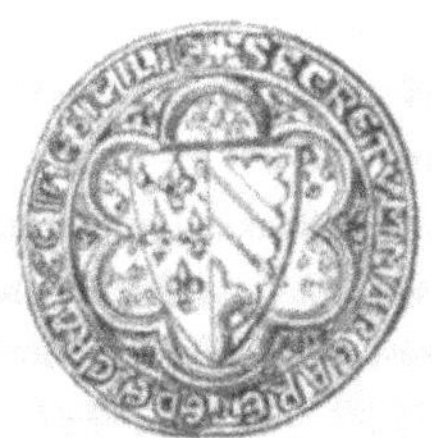

Fig. 19. Seals (1284, 1292) and counterseal of Marguerite de Bourgogne, queen of Sicily. (After Le Maistre, 1852) (Photo: Paris, Bibliothèque nationale de France).

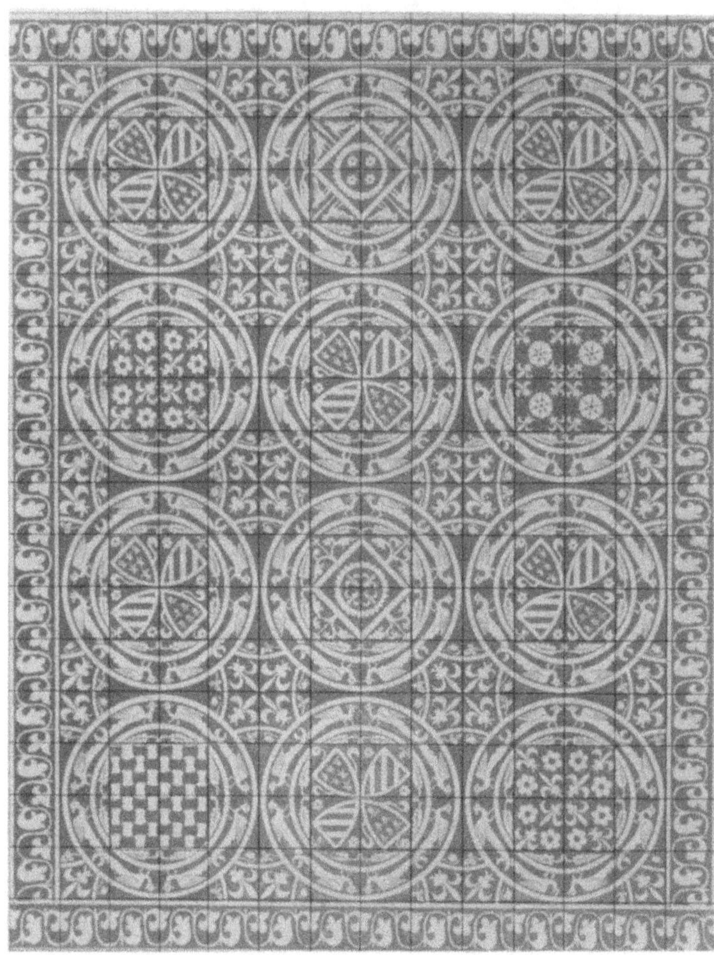

Fig. 20. Tile pavement. Tonnerre, château of Marguerite de Bourgogne, queen of Sicily. Ca. 1295. (After Amé, 1859).

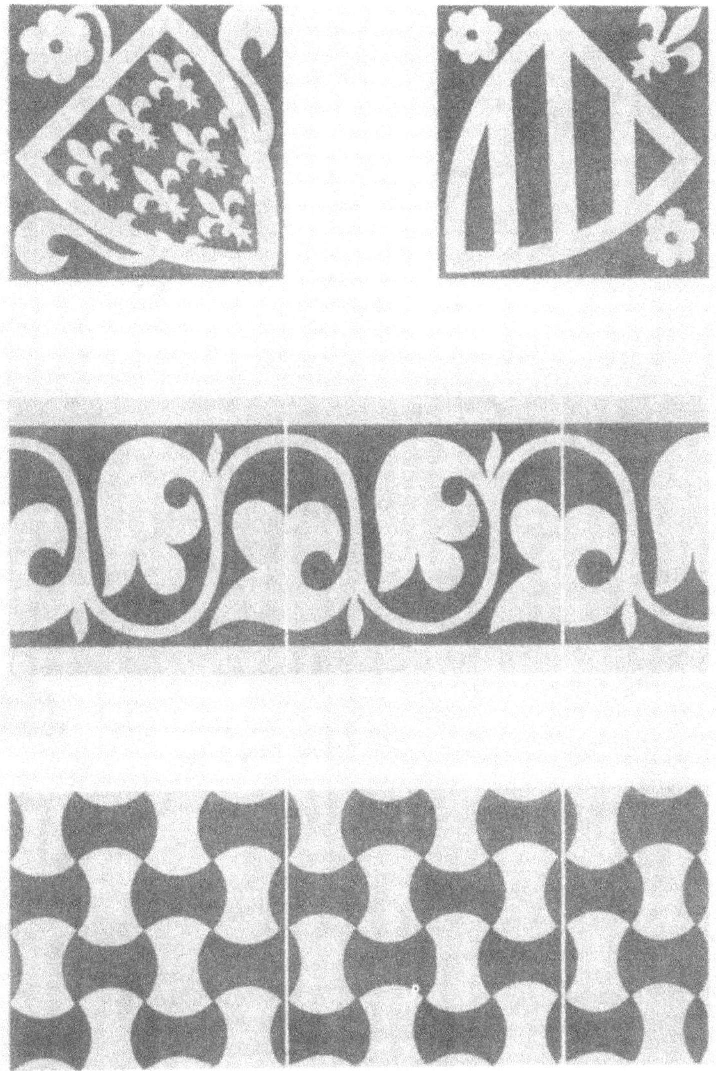

Fig. 21. Tile pavement, details of coats of arms of Burgundy and Anjou, with marguerites and fleurs de lis. Tonnerre, château of Marguerite de Bourgogne, queen of Sicily. Ca. 1295. (After Amé, 1859).

Fig. 21 con't.

There is, in the Mussy stained glass, no surviving heraldry of Anjou or Bourgogne. The three coats of arms and the fragmented inscription that Didron has installed so prominently under the band windows, however, may reveal some nuances in the picture that is emerging of the bishop's campaign of building and glazing in the years approaching 1290.

The Fragmentary Inscription

A garbled inscription band now in the center lancet of Bay 101 (Fig. 28) contains the following enigmatic letters:

:R.MINAR.T:

Fichot (Fig. 6) shows it reversed except for the T. The partial reversal suggests that in 1840 the glass was set into the window wrong-way-round (paint side out, evidence that it had been moved there), and the un-reversed, correctly set T is a reminder that each letter is on a separate piece of glass. Thus the letters of the inscription can be treated as individual survivors and only the N and A, nearly connected across the leading, must have been together originally.

The lettering style provides clues to the dating. It is much more appropriate to the late thirteenth century than to after 1300. The letters are well-spaced Lombardic capitals except for the M, which is "of a modified Roman form with the vertical strokes extended upwards," as in the inset brass lettering of the great mosaic pavement of Henry III in the presbytery of Westminster Abbey, dated 1268.[33] A generally Lombardic alphabet retaining this debased Roman M (and occasionally also N and T) appears on an Oxfordshire tomb ca. 1274 and a York Minster tomb ca. 1279. The style of inset brass lettering known as Lincolnshire 'Style A,' in use 1270-1300, also retains these Roman forms while in the more fashionable city of London, the 'Main Group' lettering in use during the 1280s and 1290s already has achieved a full Lombardic alphabet.[34]

In the context of French stained glass one can offer similar

[33] John Blair, "English Monumental Brasses Before 1350:Types, Patterns and Workshops," in *The Earliest English Brasses, Patronage, Style and Workshops 1270-1350*, ed. John Coales (London: 1987) pp. 136, 139, fig. 138C. The Mussy letter cannot be an H as reported in Recensement IV p. 148, Bay 100. The Lombardic curved h (based on minuscule h) had completely superseded Roman capital H well before the late thirteenth century.

[34] Blair pp. 140-42, fig. 148. Lincolnshire "Style B," introduced ca. 1320, has Lombardic M (Blair fig. 196A).

comparisons. Sées cathedral, where the glazing predates 1280, uses a mixed alphabet, while in the nave of Saint-Père de Chartres ca. 1305-15 one finds a fully Lombardic lettering, still well spaced but somewhat more compressed than at Mussy (such lateral compression is a later development).[35] The fully Lombardic alphabet appears at Beauvais cathedral even earlier, in the chapel window given by Raoul de Senlis ca. 1290-95, as well as in the early choir chapel donations at Evreux. A good example of a debased Roman M of the earlier era appears in the Mauclerc lancets under the south rose of Chartres, which I would date 1228.[36] Even allowing for the provincial isolation of Mussy-sur-Seine, the lettering of its fragmentary inscription strongly suggests a dating no later than 1290.

The archaic Roman M seems to have been chosen by the glazier to achieve a nice visual accent. Thus for a reconstruction of the inscription I would suggest:

M[A]R[...] R[EGINA] T[ORNODORI] [DOM]INA
(Queen Marguerite Lady of Tonnerre)

Of course the original inscription could have been much, much longer, approximating her full title as it appears on her widow's seal (of which two exemplars are known from 1292, Fig. 19):[37]

MARGARETA, DEI GRATIA JERUSALEM ET SICILIAE REGINA, TORNODORI COMITISSA, CENOMANI, MONTISMIRI ET ALODIAE DOMINA

The question of the original location of the inscription in the glass, and the period of its mutilation, will be addressed at the conclusion of this study.

---

[35] On Sées: Lillich, *Armor* p. 198. On Saint-Père: Lillich, *Saint-Père* pls. 55, 56, 63-64, 74 and color pl. VII.

[36] Beauvais: Grodecki and Brisac, *Le Vitrail gothique* fig. 147. Evreux: Marcel Baudot, "Les Verrières de la cathédrale d'Evreux: cinq siècles d'histoire," *Nouvelles de l'Eure* no. 27 (1966) ill. pp. 28-29 (Louis de France and Marguerite d'Artois, married 1300). The Mauclerc lancet in question (S' MATh'S) is illustrated in Jean Rollet, *Les Maîtres de la lumière* (Paris: 1980) p. 165. For the date of the Chartres south rose see Lillich, "Early Heraldry: How to Crack the Code," *Gesta* XXX/1 (1991) pp. 43-44.

[37] Le Maistre (1852-53) pp. 146-47; Douët-d'Arcq no. 11766.

Bishop Gui and the Coat of Arms of Vienne

Bishop Gui was one of seven sons of the count of Geneva, all but two of whom were high-ranking churchmen and all but one of whom predeceased him. His once close-knit family, by the last years of his long episcopate, amounted to far-flung distant relations.[38] His nephew Aymon III, count of Geneva (d. 1290), had only two daughters, born between 1271-79: Jeanne de Genève, second wife of Philippe de Vienne (d. 1312), a familiar of the duke of Burgundy; and Contesson de Genève, who married Philippe's younger brother Jean. I will return to them shortly.

Gui, who reigned as bishop of Langres for a quarter century, was as son of the count of Geneva well connected with the ruling aristocracy of his era. The duke of Burgundy addressed him as *cousin*; Edmund, count of Lancaster and brother to the English king, called him *consanguineo nostro*; and Philippe le Bel referred to him as *fidèle et parent*.[39] Gui had been present at the death of St Louis in Tunis and accompanied Philippe le Hardi on the sad journey home. King Philippe spent eighteen days at Christmas 1274 at Gui's château in Mussy.[40] The bishop served him as counselor, *précepteur* of his children, and as one of the king's testa-mentary executors named in 1284.[41] The following year Gui accompanied his monarch on the ill-fated *chevauchée d'Aragon* and was with him in Perpignan when he died. Philippe le Bel, en route home with his father's body, gave Bishop Gui a donation of land 'to recognize the zeal with which he had served his father during his illness.'[42] He also served this king as *conseilleur*.[43]

One has Matthew Paris's word that the bishopric of Langres was not wealthy ("episcopus Lingonensis, qui si pauper sit...") and bulls of Boniface VIII establishing that Bishop Gui was notably in debt when he

[38] Anselme II, pp. 158-59. Gui de Genève's eldest brother Rodolphe, count of Geneva, died by 1275 as did Amé, bishop of Die; Henri, the other layman, seems to have died before 1273, and Aymon, *chantre* of Geneva, by 1270; Robert, bishop of Geneva, died 1288. Only Jean, bishop of Valence, survived Gui, dying in 1297/98.

[39] Anselme II, p. 155; Mathieu, 117; Ernest Petit, *Histoire des ducs de Bourgogne de la race capétienne* VI (Dijon: 1898), 74, p. 336 no. 4741.

[40] Lambert, 97.

[41] Mathieu, 115; Anselme II, p. 155; Petit, *Histoire* VI, pp. 72-73.

[42] Petit, *Histoire* VI, p. 74, charters no. 4715 (Narbonne), no. 4741 (Château-Thierry), no. 4748 (Paris).

[43] Mathieu , 121.

died in 1291.[44] It seems likely that his construction of Mussy was at least partly responsible for that debt, while the embellishment of its stained glass with royal borders is no more than what one would expect from the king's aged tutor.

As at Le Mans cathedral[45] and no doubt many other places, the bishop seems to have turned to his family for contributions to his glazing project. The shield now installed at Mussy in Bay 100 (Fig. 22) displays the coat of arms of Vienne, *de gueules à l'aigle d'or* (Figs. 23-24), as has been recognized without explanation of how such a donation might have come about.[46] The gift was probably from the bishop's grandniece Jeanne, who had married Philippe de Vienne in the early 1280s, or possibly from Jeanne and her sister Contesson together using the arms of the house into which they had both married.[47] The gift may not have been large. Philippe de Vienne, whom a regional historian has labeled "un des plus remuants barons de nos contrées," badly needed money in the 1280s and early '90s.[48]

The Rochefort Coat of Arms

Another coat of arms in the Mussy glass, installed by Didron in Bay 102, displays *d'argent au lion de gueules* (Fig. 25). This shield was not included by Fichot in his watercolor of 1840, which suggests that at that

[44] Matthew Paris, *Chronica Majora* V, ed. Henry Richard Luard, Rerum Britannicorum Medii Aevi Scriptores (Rolls Series) 57 (London: 1880, rpt. Wiesbaden: 1964) p. 606. For Boniface's bulls see Petit, *Histoire* VI p. 150, charters p. 531 nos. 5927-5929.

[45] On the stained glass gifts of the kin of Bishop Geoffroy de Loudun in Le Mans cathedral: Lillich, "The Consecration of 1254: Heraldry and History in the Windows of Le Mans Cathedral," *Traditio* XXXVIII (1982) pp. 344-52.

[46] Pinto pp. 78-79; Recensement IV p. 147.

[47] Jean de Vienne's arms were differenced by a *lambel.* On the arms used by Philippe and Jean de Vienne: Max Prinet, "Sceaux franc-comtois décrits dans un ouvrage de sigillographie dauphinoise," *Académie des sciences, belles-lettres et arts de Besançon, Procès-verbaux et Mémoires* [no volume no.] (1907) pp. 154-59. See also Douët-d'Arcq nos. 3869, 3874, 3875; Coulon p. 89 no. 522; Walter de Gray Birch, *Catalogue of Seals in the Department of Manuscripts in the British Museum* V (London: 1898) p. 631 no. 19796; for the tinctures, see *Rolls of Arms, Henry III*, Aspilogia II (London: 1967) p. 194 (Walford's Roll no. 130). On the date of Jeanne's marriage: Philippe's first wife was probably still alive in 1280 (Petit, *Histoire* VI p. 34); Jeanne de Genève must have married him by 1285, since their fourth son Renaud was already a page in another household in 1295 (Anselme VII p. 798).

[48] Jean Richard, *Les Ducs de Bourgogne et la formation du duché du XIe au XIVe siècle* (Paris: 1954) pp. 308, 313, 358; Petit, *Histoire* VI pp. 34, 155-57, 196, charters nos. 4509, 4695, 4697, 5080, 5225.

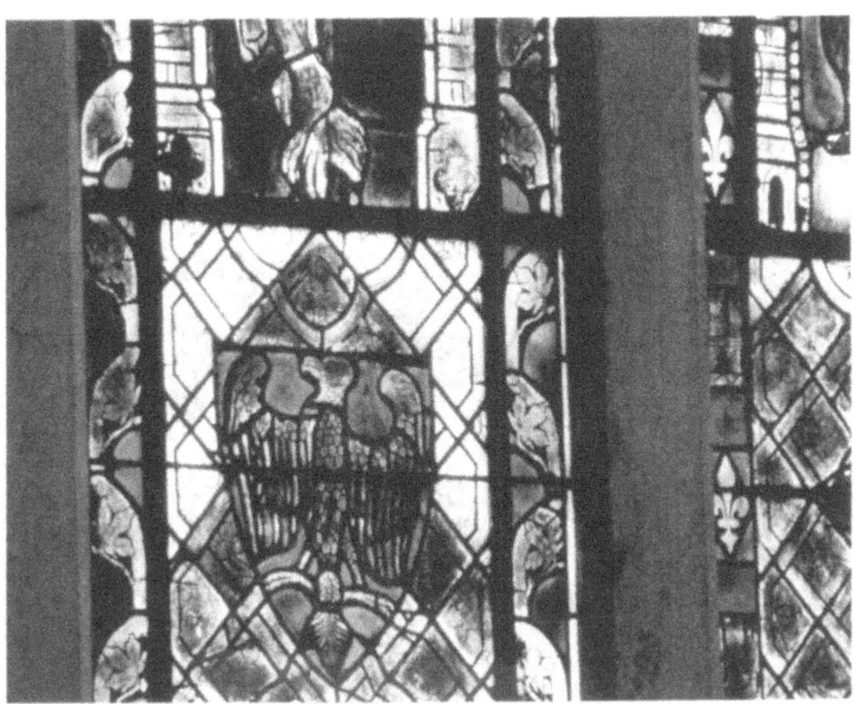

Fig. 22. Mussy. Bay 100. Arms of Vienne: *de gueules à l'aigle d'or*. Ca. 1288-93. (Photo: Lillich).

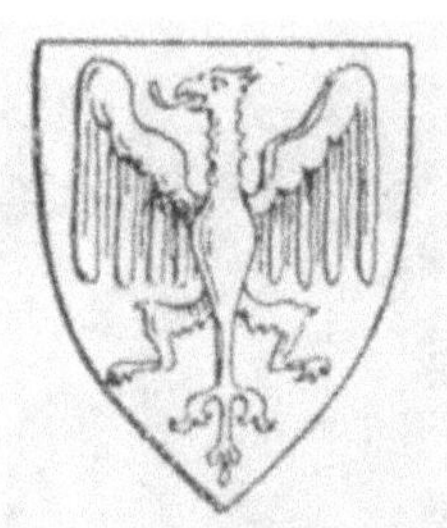

Fig. 23. Arms *à l'aigle* of the sons of Philippe de Vienne on seals, 1294 (Arch. nat. J 254 A, no. 27). (After Petit, vol. VI no. 5187).

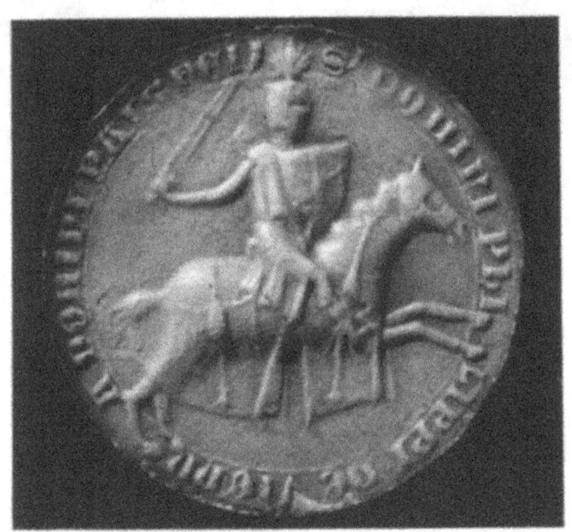

Fig. 24. Seal of Philippe de Vienne, 1294, with coat of arms *à l'aigle*. Douët-d'Arcq 3875. (Photo: Archives nationales).

time it was 'out-of-sight,' possibly in the single window of the John the Baptist chapel off the east side of the south transept, or perhaps in the lateral window of the north choir aisle (Fig. 51, Bay 7), then probably still closed off from the main sanctuary by partition walls. The 1766 plan drawn by the canon Maillefert (Fig. 50) shows the walls separating the sanctuary and aisles.[49] Pinto has noted that the shield has a damasquined ground, not otherwise found at Mussy.[50] This might indicate that it was not originally among the sanctuary glazing ensemble, but a different commission. Such decorative grounds, in which the glass is painted with a matte out of which the design is carefully removed with a blunt tool in a technique called 'stickwork,' have a long tradition in eastern France and appear at Saint-Urbain de Troyes.[51]

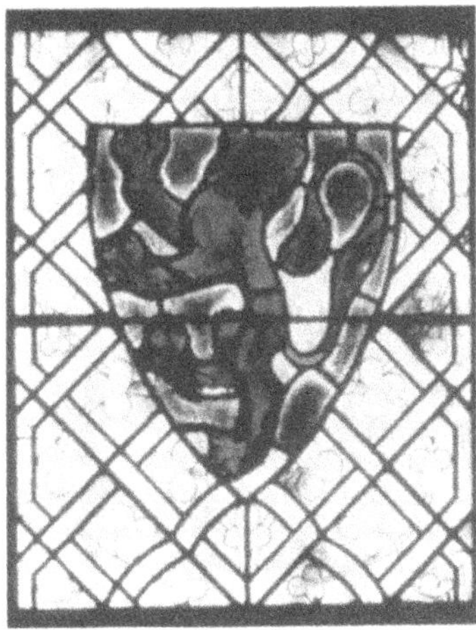

Fig. 25. Mussy. Bay 102. Arms of Rochefort: *d'argent au lion de gueules*. Ca. 1288-93; grisaille modern. (Photo: Lillich).

[49] Hier. Alex. Maillefert is among the canons whose names were engraved on the choir stalls of 1789: Pierre Dautriat, *Historique de Mussy sur Seine* (Troyes: 1955) p. 31. The 1766 plan is now among the papers of the canon Charles Nioré (Troyes, Bibl. mun. MS 3089 v. 3 fol. 1043). The closure originally was completed by the jubé (built ca. 1550, destroyed and replaced by a grill 1733), creating a collegiate choir for the canons. See Salet, "Mussy" p. 322. For the walls see Arnaud (1837) p. 224; for the jubé, Roserot, *Dictionnaire* II p. 1008 and Lambert p. 368.

[50] Pinto (thesis p. 79), noting also that the lion appears to be a modern restoration, as is the grisaille surrounding the shield.

[51] See the discussion in Lillich, *Rainbow* pp. 64-65. Examples of early fourteenth-century heraldic glass with damasquined grounds, particularly common when the field is a light color such as *or* or *argent*: *The Age of Chivalry, Art in Plantagenet England 1200-1400*, ed. Jonathan Alexander and Paul Binski (London: 1987) p. 291, sometimes dated before 1322; Peter Newton, *The County of Oxford*, Corpus Vitrearum Great Britain I (London: 1979) pp. 85-87, pl. 4c (series of shields at Dorcester, Oxon.).

The arms can most reasonably be identified as those of de Rochefort (Figs. 26, 27), family of several bishops of Langres including the ones who immediately preceded and followed Gui de Genève. His successor was Jean de Rochefort (d. 1305), consecrated bishop of Langres by 1296.[52] The arms of the Rochefort bishops are reported incorrectly by Père Anselme and Daguin. There were two families in the region by that name, and the one to which the Langres bishops belonged was Rochefort-sur-Brevon (Côte-d'Or), which used as arms a lion rampant.[53] The tinctures are

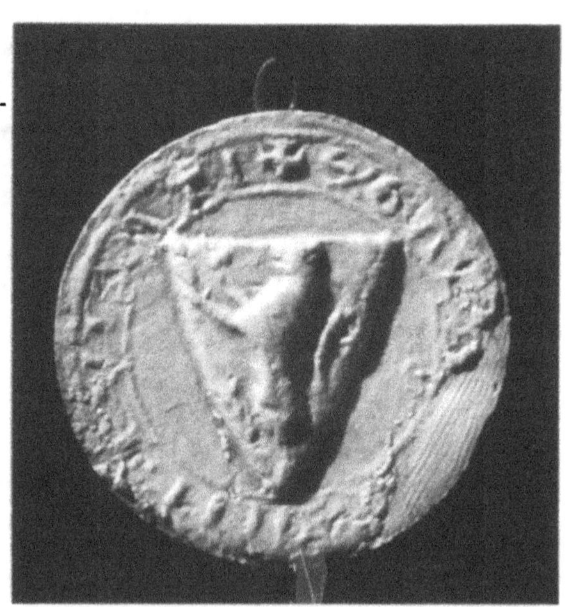

Fig. 26. Seal of Gaucher de Rochefort, 1254, with coat of arms *au lion*. Douët-d'Arcq 3415. (Photo: Archives nationales).

[52] Anselme II p. 167; Mathieu pp. 124-28; Daguin pp. 117-18; Roserot, *Dictionnaire* I p. 99; Jean-Marc Roger, "Les Morhier champenois," *Bulletin philologique et historique (jusqu'à 1610) du Comité des travaux historique et scientifique* VII (1978) pp. 101-3.

[53] Prinet, "Héraut Berry" pp. 176-77. Many Rochefort seals show the lion: Douët-d'Arcq II p. 52 no. 3415 (1254); Coulon p. 77 no. 441 (1287); Petit, *Histoire* VI p. 481 no. 5615 (1301). Bishop Jean's seal included no heraldry, but Bishop Gui de Rochefort, Jean's elder brother, had included a lion on his seals: Douët-d'Arcq no. 6621 (1254); Coulon no. 954-55 (1263). Their nephew Pierre de Rochefort used a seal with a lion shield as archdeacon of Langres (1314, Arch. Haute-Marne G 164) and as bishop (Daguin p. 124; Arch. Haute-Marne G 12 and Arch. Haute-Marne moulage no. 536, both dated 1326).

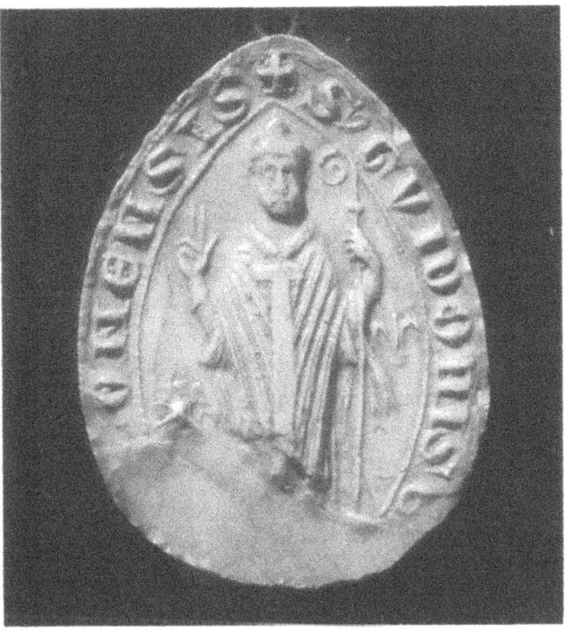

Fig. 27. Seal of Bishop Gui de Rochefort, 1254, with his family's rampant lion below his blessing hand. Douët-d'Arcq 6621. (Photo: Archives nationales).

reported in later armorials as they appear at Mussy, *gueules* on *argent*.[54] The stained glass shield of Jean de Rochefort need not date as late as 1296 when he became bishop, however. In 1250 Jean was already a canon of Langres; in 1255, possibly archdeacon; in 1279 and 1288 he held the influential post of treasurer of the chapter.[55] Brother of a previous bishop and uncle of one to come, long a trusted officer of the chapter, Jean de Rochefort would be remembered on his tomb with an elegant and touching epitaph:[56]

M. C. TER ET ANNIS CVM QVINTO VITA JOANNIS
NONIS S[=F]INITVR SEPTEMBRIS, IBI SEPELITVR

---

[54] Louvan Geliot, *La Vraye et parfaite science des armoiries*, augm. par Pierre Palliot, II (Paris: 1660, facsimile Paris: 1895) pp. 363-64: Rochefort-sur-Brenon (sic).

[55] Roger pp. 101-2. His 1255 reference is from the Vignier MS (BNF fr. 5993) and thus suspect. Roger's paragraph (p. 102) concerning the duke of Burgundy calling Bishop Gui de Rochefort *nostre cousin* is based on the Vignier manuscript and the date 1256 must be yet another of Vignier's casual errors. The charter must refer to Bishop Gui de Genève (see at n. 39 above).

[56] Daguin p. 118; cf. Mathieu pp. 127-28. Many thanks to Paul Archambault for improving my translation.

PRESVL LINGONICVS, LARGVS PIETATIS AMICVS,
INCLITVS ET LENIS, SVA SEMPER SPARSIT EGENIS,
DE SAVO FORTI, CELO DEVS ADDE COHORTI

(On the fifth of September in 1305, John's life is over, here is laid to rest the patron of Langres, generous friend of piety, re-nowned and gentle, always charitable to the poor, may God add de Rochefort to the heavenly host)

Jean de Rochefort would have had every right to expect that, when Bishop Gui de Genève's long tenure was over, the church of Mussy would be placed in his charge.

The Coat of Arms de Mussy

The shield now in Bay 101 (Fig. 28), which has been misidentified as the arms of Guillaume de Mussy (as discussed in Part I above), can be blazoned *de gueules au chef d'argent à la bande componée d'argent et de sable brochant sur le tout, à la bordure d'azur.* No other example of precisely these arms exists in any medium. The border is omitted and the tinctures of field and *chef* reversed or altered in all heraldry connected with the name de Mussy, from the late fourteenth century through Père Vignier

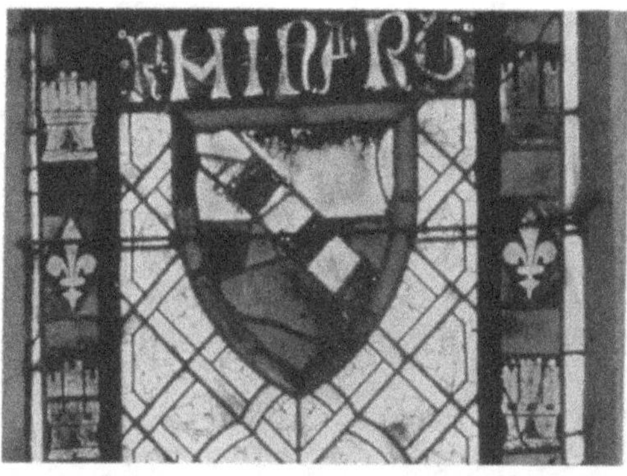

Fig. 28. Mussy. Bay 101. Fragments of an inscription; coat of arms (of Gui de Mussy?), *de gueules au chef d'argent à la bande componée d'argent et de sable brochant sur le tout, à la bordure d'azur.* Ca. 1288-93. (Photo: Lillich)

tinctures of field and *chef* reversed or altered in all heraldry connected with the name de Mussy, from the late fourteenth century through Père Vignier to the modern regional armorial compiled by Le Clert.[57]

In medieval heraldry, *brisures* such as a border or the reversal of tinctures were used to indicate that the bearer was not the head of the house. Bishop Gui de Genève, for example, reversed the tinctures of his eldest brother's arms; Charles de Valois, brother of King Philippe le Bel, used a border *gueules* on the arms of France. [58] It is fairly easy to prove that one branch of the family de Mussy, at least by the last quarter of the fourteenth century, used arms related to the stained glass at Mussy, but without the border and with altered tinctures: *d'or au chef de gueules à la bande componée d'argent et de sable brochant sur le tout.*

This family, most probably descended from Guillaume de Mussy's son Jean (see genealogy, Fig. 29), was located around Chaource and Chesley (see map Fig. 1). The arms appeared on the foot of a stone market cross in the village of Chesley.[59] Most remarkable are instances of their arms in the church of Chaource. According to an inventory of 1503 the arms decorated chasubles, tunics and copes, a gilt silver cross, and an enameled pax.[60] A now much deteriorated but fascinating sixteenth-century fresco shows a sort of visualized family tree with the arms many times repeated and the inscription "Cy gisent messire Henry de Mussy, chevalier, et dame Ysabeau de Pargues, lesquels heurent par mariage 23 enfants à savoir 13 fils et 10 filles et trespassèrent en l'an 1373."[61]

---

[57] Louis Le Clert, *Armorial historique de l'Aube* (1911, rpt. Marseille: 1976) p. 228 no. 1226.

[58] A good general introduction to such marks of cadency is ch. XXXI of Arthur Charles Fox-Davies, *A Complete Guide to Heraldry* (New York: 1978). On Bishop Gui see Daguin p. 116. On Charles de Valois, see Anselme I p. 99.

[59] Lambert p. 354, quoting Père Vignier, BNF fr. 5995 fol. 220r.

[60] Charles Lalore, *Etat de la paroise de Chaource avant la Révolution* (Arcis-sur-Aube: 1884) pp. 18, 20, 23-24, 57.

[61] The fresco, now quite damaged, bears the date 1548 and is thus commemorative. Marc Thibout, "La Peinture murale de l'église de Chaource," *Congrès archéologique* CXIII (1955) pp. 370-74. The fresco was described by a visitor to the church in 1730: see Ernest Petit, ed., "Voyage de l'abbé Lebeuf à Clairvaux en 1730," *Bulletin de la Société des sciences historiques et naturelles de l'Yonne* XLI (1887) p. 40. In his n. 1 Petit has misidentified the family, confusing them with Mussy-la-Fosse in the Côte-d'Or (see p. 54 below). The fresco was even more completely described in 1646 by Du Buisson-Aubenay, "Voyage d'un archéologue dans le sud-ouest de la Champagne en 1646," ed. Albert Babeau, *Annuaire administratif, statistique et commercial du département de l'Aube* 2e partie (1886) pp. 3-49.

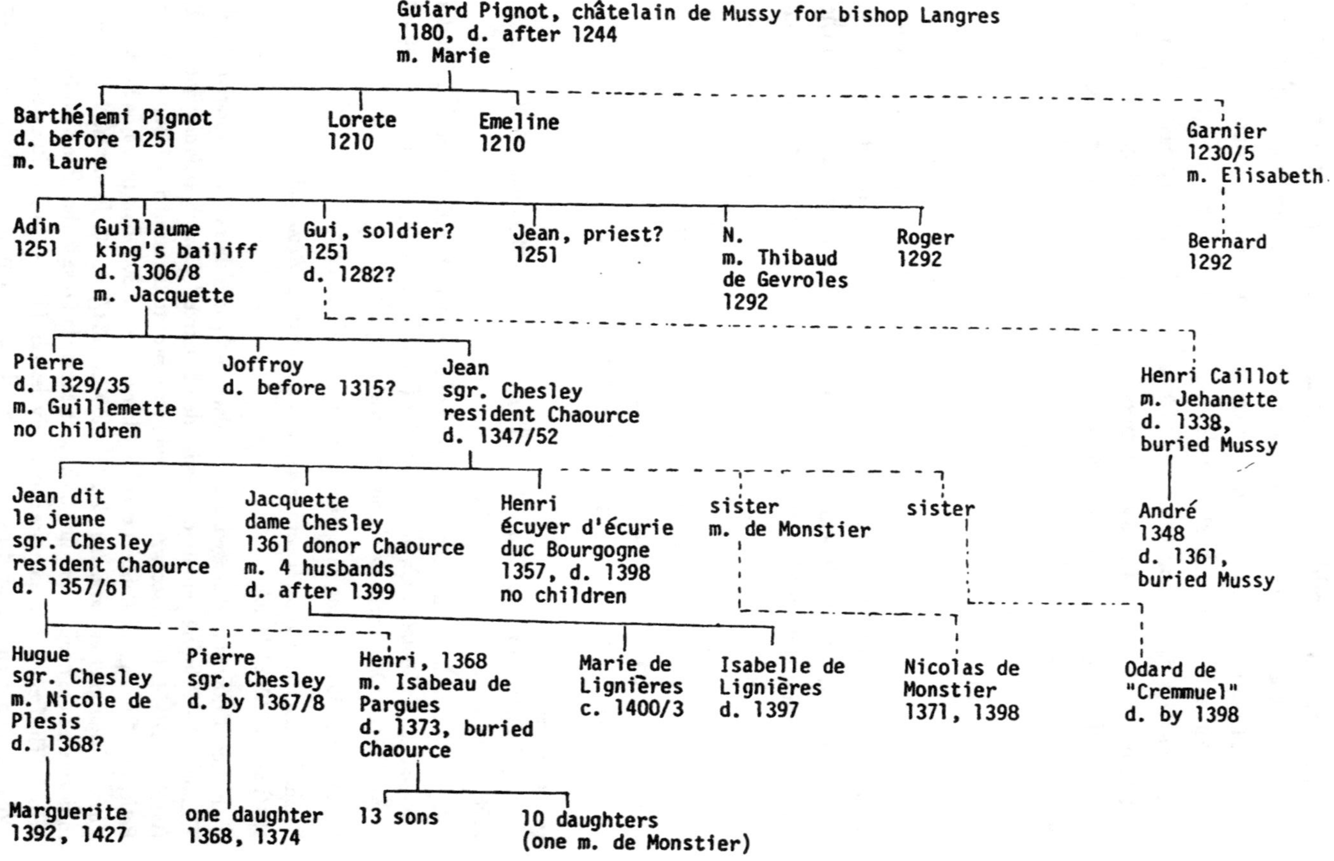

Fig. 29. Genealogical chart of the family de Mussy. Dotted lines indicate hypothetical relationship.

According to a visitor to Chaource in 1646, another inscription in the nave identified "Henry de Muxi" as the founder of a chaplaincy in 1368, and the arms also appeared in a stained glass window in the choir.[62] In the late fourteenth century the family intermarried with de Monstier, and coats of arms quarterly Monstier/Mussy appear in the chapel at Chaource in a lower part of the above-mentioned fresco, on a fifteenth-century altar retable (Fig. 30), and in stained glass of ca. 1545.[63]

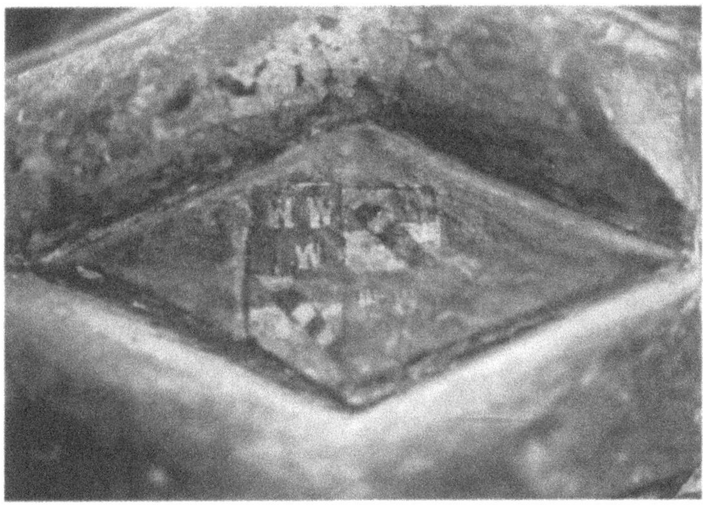

Fig. 30. Chaource (Aube), Saint-Jean-Baptiste. Painted stone altarpiece, 15th century, with arms quarterly Monstier and Mussy (*d'or au chef de gueules à la bande componée d'argent et de sable brochant sur le tout*). (Photo: Lillich).

[62] Du Buisson-Aubenay pp. 45-46.

[63] The painted stone retable, depicting the Crucifixion and martyrdom scenes, is mentioned briefly by Francis Salet, "L'Eglise de Chaource," *Congrès archéologique* CXIII (1955), 367; and in "Chaource," *La Vie en Champagne*, 28e année, no. 300 spécial (June 1980) unpaginated (see "La Chapelle Saint-Georges"). On the stained glass see Recensement IV p. 72 (Bay 10).

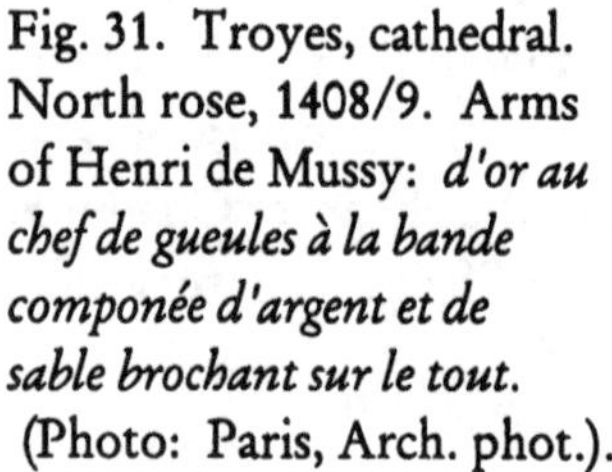

Fig. 31. Troyes, cathedral. North rose, 1408/9. Arms of Henri de Mussy: *d'or au chef de gueules à la bande componée d'argent et de sable brochant sur le tout.* (Photo: Paris, Arch. phot.).

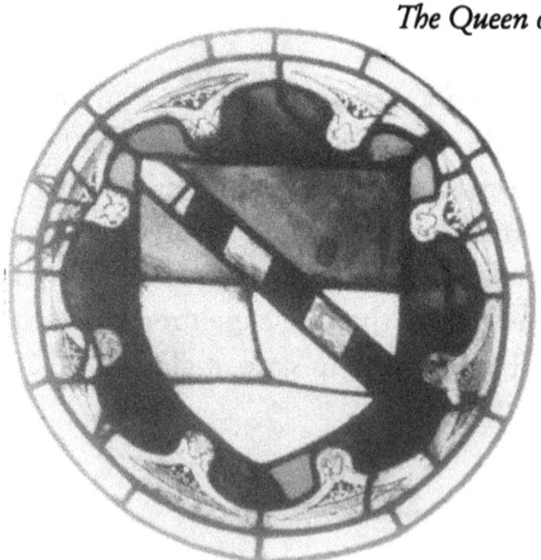

Yet another stained glass example of these Mussy arms appears in the upper left corner of the north rose of Troyes cathedral (Fig. 31), which was reglazed in 1408/9 following a collapse in 1390.[64] The contract specifies, for the rose's four spandrels, the evangelists accompanied by eight shields, the heraldry to be provided to the glazier by the chapter. Though now severely damaged, the arms include France, Navarre, the chapter of Troyes, an earlier bishop of Troyes (Jean d'Auxois, reigned 1342-52), and Henri de Mussy. Fichot connected these arms with the Henri de Mussy he found in a charter of 1370, who—he says—had a house in Troyes and was a man of substance, *seigneur* of Bierne and Savoie in the Aube, governor of the château of Beaufort (Montmorency near Chavanges) and *maître d'hôtel* of the Burgundian duke Philippe le Hardi.[65] Two seals exist, of 1383 (Fig. 32) and 1391, for this Henri de Mussy,[66] who actually served the duke of Burgundy as *écuyer d'écurie.*

---

[64] Recensement IV p. 231, bay 219; Stephen Murray, *Building Troyes Cathedral, The Late Gothic Campaigns* (Bloomington, Ind.: 1987) pp. 56-59, 140. This rose had been glazed 1375/76 but was badly damaged in 1390 and reglazed "tout a neuf." The Mussy shield was in the lower right corner when Fichot described it, and the arms are not *coupé* as he blazons them: Charles Fichot, *Statistique monumentale du département de l'Aube* III (Troyes: 1894) p. 279.

[65] Fichot p. 279. His reference for the charter (Arch. Aube E 152, registre) is incorrect, as was noted by Charles Nioré, "La Rosace du portail nord à la cathédrale de Troyes," *La Revue catholique, semaine religieuse de la ville et du diocèse de Troyes* XXXVII no. 28 (14 July 1900) p. 452 n. 2.

[66] Seal of 1383: Germain Demay, *Inventaire des sceaux de la collection Clairambault à la Bibliothèque nationale* I (Paris: 1885) pp. 697-98 no. 6615. Seal of 1391: Arch. Aube, Layette 40 H 1, donation 29/1/1391 by Henri de Mussi escuyer for his anniversary to Hôtel-Dieu-le-Comte, Troyes; this seal also survives as a cast, Arch. Haute-Marne moulage no. 203. On the cast, one of a group made by Paul de Fleury, see Charles-François Roussel, *Le Diocèse de Langres, histoire et statistique* I (Langres: 1873) p. 392.

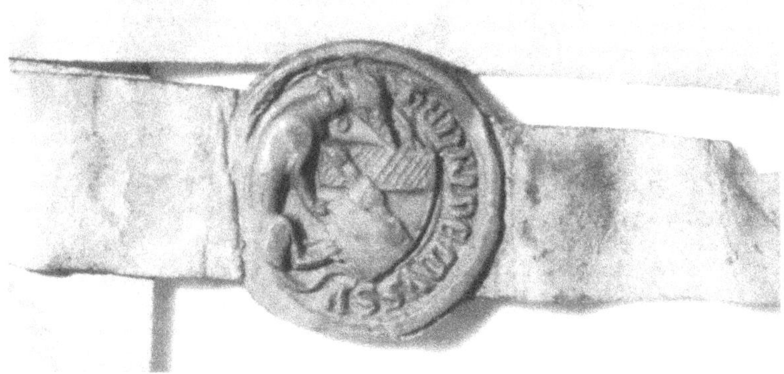

Fig. 32. Seal of Henri de Mussy, 1383, with coat of arms *au chef à la bande componée brochant sur le tout* (19 mm., Paris, BNF Clairambault r. 79 p. 6239, no. 187, Demay 6615). (Photo: Paris, Bibliothèque nationale de France).

He appears in charters by 1357 and died 1398/9, without surviving wife or children. Henri's sister was Jacquette de Mussy, married four times, who founded a chaplaincy at Chaource in 1361; their elder brother was Jean de Mussy *dit le jeune* (see genealogical chart, Fig. 29).[67] These three siblings are probably the children of Jean de Mussy, Guillaume de Mussy's son. In 1329 Jean senior—as well as his son Jean—were living in towers of the château of Chaource, and he owned land in Chesley which passed to a Pierre de Mussy, by 1368-74 to his widow, and by 1383 to the much-married Jacquette mentioned above.[68] She may have been named for her grandmother, Guillaume de Mussy's wife Jacquette, but it is noteworthy that no member of the clan ever again bore the name of Guillaume—a judgment passed upon the corrupt king's bailiff by his own kin.

---

[67] Roserot, *Dictionnaire* I pp. 178-79 (Bierne), p. 473 (Cussangy). On Jacquette de Mussy see Anselme VI p. 733, VIII p. 837.

[68] Roserot, *Dictionnaire* I p. 383 (Chesley), II p. 566 (Etourvy); Auguste Longnon, *Documents relatifs au comté de Champagne et de Brie, 1172-1361* II (Paris: 1901-14) pp. 397-99, 401, 408-10. Bautier places the death of Jean senior between 1347-52: Bautier p. 93 n. 4 (cf. p. 90 n. 4). Roserot's assertions that he was married to Guillemette de Pommard and dead ca. 1361 may be questioned. His sources may have been charters in Petit, *Histoire* IX nos. 8835 (1355), 9359 and 9361 (1361). Pommard and Savigny-sous-Beaune, mentioned in the 1355 charter, are in southernmost Burgundy below Dijon, and it is not established whether these charters refer to the Jean de Mussy in question or to Jean de Mussy[-la-Fosse] (see below p. 54).

De Mussy Arms at Mussy-sur-Seine

The false hypothesis of Guillaume de Mussy as founder, exploded in Part I, rested on the assumption that the arms in the stained glass were his. In the mid seventeenth century Père Vignier, in his attempt to establish his mythical crusading ancestor as founder, had observed further (BNF fr. 5994 fol. 270v):[69]

> On voit qu'il a été fondateur, que ses armes étaient celles qui se voient aux clefs de la voûte, et que l'effigie du chevalier qui est représenté dans les vitres avec sa cotte d'armes, et sur sa sépulture qui est dans le choeur à côté du grand autel, est la sienne.
> (One sees that he was the founder, that his arms were those that appear on the vault keystones, and that the image of the knight who is represented in the windows with his heraldic surcoat, and on his tomb which is in the choir beside the high altar, is his.)

On fol. 272r Vignier noted: "The arms of de Mussy are of *gueules au chef d'or, à la bande componée de sable et d'argent de six pièces....*" Vignier was, as Pinoteau characterized another seventeenth-century author, "*un grand imaginatif* who nonetheless sometimes had good information."[70] What data has Vignier provided that one can work with?

Vignier mentions three coats of arms 'de Mussy' that he saw in the church: on a vault keystone, on the heraldic surcoat of a knight depicted in the stained glass, and on a tomb next to the high altar. And he blazons the arms in question similarly to the surviving stained glass shield (Fig. 28), which is mentioned specifically neither by Vignier nor de La Brosse. If one takes the leap of faith and assumes that the surviving shield did indeed accompany the lost glassy knight in heraldic surcoat described in the seventeenth-century documents, how does Vignier's blazon compare? He makes the *chef or* and not *argent*; this would be a possible mistake because the white glass has weathered to a dull tan, and seems originally to have been covered with a now deteriorated wash (picked out with some emblem or pattern that is now impossible to read, at least until the glass is dismounted and on the light table). Vignier reversed the *com-*

[69] Lambert publishes the Vignier texts pp. 353-54. I have substituted folio numbers for his page references, as Vignier's pagination is not consecutive and often totally confused.

[70] Hervé Pinoteau, describing the heraldist André Favyn (1620), in *L'Héraldique de Saint Louis et de ses compagnons*, Les Cahiers nobles no. 27 (Paris: 1966) p. 36.

ponée, which is probably not significant. And he omitted any mention of the *bordure d'azur*.

Is there any check on his observation of these three shields? Nothing further can be added concerning the lost kneeling knight that he saw in the choir window.[71] The tomb (Fig. 33) survives but has lost its heraldry; it will be investigated below. The vault keystone mentioned by Vignier is the only witness to provide a check on his observational powers. It is still visible in the nave (second bay from the west), though now crudely overpainted,[72] and it was drawn in 1840 by Fichot (Fig. 6 no. 5).[73] His

---

[71] While I have been unable to find evidence substantiating Bautier's statement (as in p. 4 n.8 above) p. 95 n. 2, that the window survived into the eighteenth century, it seems probable that its destruction occurred in the Revolution. See p.103 below.

[72] Armorial keystones are noted by Lambert pp. 366-71 and Arnaud p. 224. They have now been painted over with little regard for the original tinctures, though the charges can be made out in low relief. Besides those recorded in Fichot's watercolor (see n. 73 below), there are the following:
— south nave aisle, east bay: *3 jumelles?* (Villebéon)
— south nave aisle, 3rd bay from crossing: impaled, dexter a *fasce*, charged with 2 objects, between a chevron *en chef* and an object *en pointe*; sinister, a dimidiated *sautoir* (unidentified)
— chapel off south nave aisle, 2nd bay from crossing: shield now painted blue
Salet, "Mussy" pp. 321-24 notes that the keystones of the nave and transepts are armorial while those in the choir have foliage. One might compare this arrangement to Westminster Abbey, where heraldic sculptures decorate the nave while the bosses in the choir are foliage, "perhaps signifying the verdancy of paradise": T. A. Heslop, "The Iconography of the Angel Choir at Lincoln Cathedral," in *Medieval Architecture and its Intellectual Context*, ed. Eric Fernie and Paul Crossley (London: 1990) p. 156. Is this perhaps one more English detail in the architecture of Mussy? (See above, p.2).

[73] Fichot's watercolor includes the following shields:
no. 1: stained glass, now in Bay 101 (see p.46ff.)
no. 2: stained glass, now in Bay 100 (see pp. 40-42)
no. 3: stained glass, lost (see pp. 76-77)
no. 4: keystone, north nave aisle, 2nd bay from west, unidentified
no. 5: nave keystone, 3rd bay from crossing, discussed here
no. 6: nave keystone, 2nd bay from crossing, arms of the bishops of Langres (see pp. 11-13)
no. 7: nave keystone, at crossing: a *sautoir* (of bishops of Langres?) with *brochant* a sort of two-part *gonfanon?*
no. 8, "au bas d'une figure de père Eternel": shield on a fifteenth-century sculpture of the Gnadenstuhl Trinity, now in the north transept, illustrated in André Marsat, *Eglises de l'Aube* II (Paris: 1977) p. 21. The arms of no. 8 (*azur, un cerf passant d'or*) are those of the family Travaillot, used on monuments at Langres cathedral in the fifteenth century by several canons of that family: see Henry Brocard, "Inventaire des reliques et autres

drawing has a *bordure d'azur* like the surviving stained glass shield; the compony is reversed (starting with *sable* as in Vignier's blazon) and of 7, though such variations would not be important in medieval heraldry. The quatrefoils decorating the *compons sables* may just be a liberty of the artist (Fichot or the one who painted, or repainted, the keystone). And the field of the arms, as in the window, is *gueules*. The *chef* is clearly indicated in relief on the existing keystone, though its original color was apparently lost by Fichot's time. These two coats of arms could perhaps be considered as identical. One can have some faith that Vignier's three examples did indeed present the same family arms. The landscape that emerges is comparable to the church of Chaource, embellished by donations and funerary memorials of another branch of the de Mussy family.

Some Complicated and Tentative Genealogy

The problem initially is worstened by the existence of another town in the region named Mussy: Mussy-la-Fosse (Côte-d'Or), *ancien bailliage* of Semur-en-Auxois, canton of Flavigny.[74] The lords of Mussy-la-Fosse appear in late thirteenth- and in fourteenth-century records, and in 1294 there was even a chevalier Guillaume de Mussy[-la-Fosse], recently deceased, with a son of the same name (Jean) as one of Guillaume de Mussy's sons. Historians not surprisingly have confused the charters of these two families regularly. The heraldry of Mussy-la-Fosse, at least on mid fourteenth-century seals, was completely different: *une fasce à la bordure denchée.*[75]

curiosités de l'église cathédrale de Langres dressé le 30 août 1768," *Bulletin de la Société historique et archéologique de Langres* I (1880) pp. 160, 172.

[74] Lambert p. 7.

[75] A 1294 charter mentioning Guillaume de Mussy [-la-Fosse], recently dead, and his son Jean: Petit, *Histoire* VI p. 408 no. 5196 (cartulary of Fontenay). Members of the family Mussy-la-Fosse:

Eudes de Mussy, *capitaine* at the château of Montbard, known from 1352-60: Petit, *Histoire* IX, *pièces justificatives* nos. 8716, 8869, 8870, 9022, 9093, 9167, 9309; Coulon p. 71 no. 401; cf. Lambert p. 177 (1359).

Jean de Mussy, sire of Jours, châtelain of Montréal and Châtel-Girard, 1359; Petit, *Histoire* IX no. 9078; cf. Lambert p. 177 (1261 [sic?], 1359).

Philippe de Mussy, d. 1396 in Hungary, *chambellan* of the duke of Burgundy and châtelain of his château of Juilly, married (to add to the confusion!) to Marguerite de Mussy [-l'Evêque] (daughter of Hugue de Mussy and granddaughter of Jean de Mussy *dit le jeune*, see genealogical chart, Fig. 29); Coulon p. 71 no. 402; Roserot, *Dictionnaire* I

Our Guillaume de Mussy had an elder brother Adin and at least three other brothers born around the 1240's, including one named Jean (see chart, Fig. 29).[76] Nothing is known of Adin. According to Vignier his brother Jean was a parish priest. He is probably not the canon of Langres named Jean de Mussy who used a quite different coat of arms ca. 1314-18, *de gueules au lion d'or.*[77]

Guillaume and Jean had a brother Gui who disappears from regional charters, but who, I propose, may be identified as the Guillotus de Mussy who, in 1278, was a soldier in Charles d'Anjou's army in Naples—and thus probably was killed in the Sicilian Vespers 1282.[78] It might be interpolated here that, since there is no evidence that the de Mussy family was armigerous in the thirteenth century, the soldier Gui would have been the only one of his brothers who had a real need for a coat of arms. And this I believe is significant.

Considering the flimsiness of the evidence above, it is pure conjecture on my part—in the genealogical chart Fig. 29—to assign descendants to Guillaume's brother Gui. In late 1292, at the moment of

---

p. 473; cf. Lambert, 178 (1391).

[76] Guillaume and three brothers, all minors but Adin, appear in a charter of 1251, when their mother was a widow: Lambert, 529. On his brother Roger, not mentioned in the 1251 charter, see n. 79 below.

[77] Vignier stated that brother Jean was parish priest of Bligny, witnessed a charter with brother Guillaume in 1297, and made a donation to the Temple 1299: BNF fr. 5995 fol. 196v, as cited in Bautier, 66 n. 2 and p. 77.

On the canons of Langres Henri de Mussy (ca. 1240), Jean de Mussy (1280, 1320) and his brother Jacques de Mussy (1280, 1306) see: Roussel, *Le Diocèse de Langres* IV, pp. 78-80; Charles Lalore, "Chartes de l'abbaye de Mores," *Mémoires de la Société académique d'agriculture, des sciences, arts et belles-lettres du département de l'Aube* XXXVII (3e série v. X) (1873): 38-39 (obituaire). Canons Jean and Jacques had a brother, the canon Richard de Grandvilliers, as well as uncles Jean and Raoul de Mussy. Richard de Grandvilliers was one of the administrators of the see *sede vacante* 1291-96: Daguin, 117. Canon Jacques' seals show him kneeling, without heraldry. On the arms used by canon Jean de Mussy ca. 1314: G. G., "Armoiries d'anciens chanoines de Langres (suite)," *La Haute-Marne, Revue historique, archéologique et philologique* 1re année (1903-4), 194. See also Lambert, 99, 177 (as 1340). A moulage of his 1318 seal survives, in which the lion is passant or perhaps statant (*lion léopardé*): Arch. Haute-Marne moulage, 139; Coulon's typed list no. 1542 (see Part I n. 16 above). I would like to thank Lionel Gallois of the Arch. Haute-Marne for his gracious help in locating the moulage and having it photographed for me. Yet another, later canon named Jean de Mussy founded a chapel in Mussy-sur-Seine in 1368: Lambert, 364. His relationship to the family is unknown.

[78] Paul Durrieu, *Les Archives angevines de Naples, étude sur les registres du roi Charles Ier (1265-1285)* II (Paris: 1887), 356.

Guillaume's disgrace, his pledges before the court included his brother-in-law, his brother Roger (Bautier read his name as Reg...), and Bernard de Mussy, whom Bautier theorized was his cousin.[79] The progeny could as easily be Roger's or even Bernard's. I have theorized that the descendants were the soldier Gui's because, as donors, they were memorialized in the church of Mussy—as, I believe, was Gui.

Guillaume de Mussy and his wife Jacquette had at least three sons, Pierre, Joffroy and Jean de Mussy (see chart, Fig. 29). Vignier is the source for the information that the eldest was also called Perrinet (Perroz, Perrault) de Châtillon.[80] Joffroy, also according to Vignier, was alive in 1308; he was probably dead by 1315 when, after an extended inquiry motivated by antipathy to their late father, his brothers Pierre and Jean finally received royal *lettres confirmatives de noblesse*.[81] The eldest, Pierre, who married but had no children, concentrated his lavish donations on his foundation of the charterhouse in Troyes (1319, 1329), was forced by Parlement in 1322 to return a *terre* to one of his father's complaining victims, made his will in 1329, and died by 1335.[82] His brother Jean was his chief beneficiary.

Although the progeny of Jean, at Chaource, have been discussed above, the picture of him is not altogether clear. In addition to confusion with Jean de Mussy[-la-Fosse], there is a puzzling document of 1334 (Arch. nat. X^{1C} 1^{B} no. 266, Accord of Parlement) concerning a dispute over inheritance between three mysterious siblings with names very close

---

[79] Edgard Boutaric, ed., *Actes du Parlement de Paris* I (Paris: 1863) p. 275 no. 2787; Bautier, genealogical chart (after p. 66) and p. 75.

[80] BNF fr. 5994 fols. 269v, 271v. On Pierre see n. 82 below.

[81] Vignier (BNF fr. 5994 fol. 269v) is the only source for the document naming Joffroy; he gives the date as 1308, not 1303 as reported in Bautier p. 88 n. 3. On the *lettres confirmatives de noblesse* see Bautier p. 87.

[82] Bautier pp. 88-90. Pierre de Mussy's sobriquet of Châtillon, dated 1299, is reported only by Vignier: Jacques Vignier, *Décade historique du diocèse de Langres* II (Langres: 1894) p. 151 (on this publication see Appendix I below, pp. 113-14). His father Guillaume de Mussy evidently owned land in Châtillon, since his donation charter of 1287 was issued there: Lambert pp. 537-38. There was an impressive château in Châtillon-sur-Seine (see Fig. 1 above) later owned by someone named Jean de Mussy, which in 1361 served as the locus for an homage owed the bishop of Langres by the duke of Burgundy: Petit, *Histoire* IX p. 437 no. 9361. Whether the owner Jean de Mussy was Pierre's brother and heir—or someone from the family Mussy-la-Fosse—I have been unable to establish.

to those of Guillaume's three sons:[83]

> Acorde est entre Iefroy filz feu guillm' andrie de mussi / & Ieh' li gentis hons / ses freres dune part / Et perrote # fame feu Iehn' de la vacherie seur des dessus diz dautre part /—que de tous des descors / quereles & controuuersies quilont # ou peuent avoir lune partie contre lautre par quelconque cause & en quelque maniere que ce soit / Noble homme & saige mes' # Ieh' de mussi chlr' & sires henriz caillez dou dit / mussi... puissent cognoistre dire sentencier prononc' orden' ....
>
> (It is agreed between Joffroy, son of the late Guillaume André de Mussy, and the nobleman Jean, his brother, on the one hand, and Perrotte, wife of the late Jean de la Vacherie, [and] sister of the above-mentioned, on the other—that of all discords, quarrels and controversies that have or can have one side against the other, by whatever cause and in whatever kind it might be, the noble and wise man Messire Jean de Mussy knight and Sire Henri Caillot of the said Mussy... would be able to investigate to pass sentence, judgment, order ....)

The unknown Joffroy, Jean and their widowed sister Perrotte, children of a deceased Guillaume André de Mussy, chose as arbiters of their dispute Sire Henri Caillot de Mussy and the chevalier Jean de Mussy. Thus in 1334 there were at least two adult individuals named Jean de Mussy, one Guillaume's son and the other, son of Guillaume André, friend or more probably kin.

Indeed I believe it likely that the second arbiter, Henri Caillot, was also a kinsman. Les Caillots (see Fig. 1) later belonged to various individuals named de Mussy, and Henri may have been called Caillot just as Pierre de Mussy was called Châtillon, probably after an important residence.[84] And Henri seems to have been established as a family name (see genealogical chart, Fig. 29). About Henri Caillot de Mussy there are some data. He rented a house in Mussy owned by the bishop, witnessed Pierre de Mussy's will in 1329,[85] died in 1338 and was buried with his wife in the church of Mussy-sur-Seine, according to a long inscription plaque

---

[83] Thanks to Paul Archambault for improving my translation. I owe the transcription to the kindness of Elizabeth A. R. Brown, to whom I am extremely grateful. The document is mentioned in Roserot, *Dictionnaire* II p. 1007 and Bautier p. 96 n. 4. Guillaume André (not on my chart Fig. 29) was probably a nephew of Guillaume de Mussy and cousin to the knight Jean and Henri Caillot.

[84] On Les Caillots: Roserot, *Dictionnaire* I p. 272. On Pierre 'de Châtillon' see n. 82 above.

[85] Lambert pp. 372-73; Bautier p. 96 n. 4.

provided by their son André (d. 1361) and now set into the south transept wall. The inscription will be discussed below. Indeed it has been suggested that the surviving gisant tomb of the founders which was mentioned earlier (Fig. 33) is that of Henri Caillot de Mussy[86]—and I believe that it is.

The Founders' Tomb

Now in the north transept, an immense tomb formed from a single monolithic slab presents gisant figures of an anonymous knight and his wife (Fig. 33). It would certainly have been a difficult stone to carve and the workmanship is local and maladroit. This tomb[87] was seen by Vignier around 1650 in the choir next to the high altar; it was placed upright against the sanctuary wall probably ca. 1740, and moved to the present location in the nineteenth century. Vignier reported that it had a coat of arms 'de Mussy' that had been effaced by 1837 and by 1878 was lost altogether. Lambert reports that the tomb was always known as that of the (unnamed) founders.[88]

The identity of the couple has been hotly debated. Following Vignier's fanciful identification with his imaginary crusading ancestor, recent opinions have settled on either Guillaume de Mussy (d. 1306/8) and his wife Jacquette or Henri Caillot de Mussy (d. 1338) and wife Jeannette. While Bautier (p. 96) investigated comparisons in books on the history of costume, no-one has compared the gisants to other medieval tombs—and art historians have long known that funerary art is notoriously old-fashioned. This study will attempt such comparisons based on the

---

[86] Lucien Morel-Payen, *Troyes et l'Aube* (Paris: 1929), 201; Jacques Laurent and Ferdinand Claudon, *Abbayes et prieurés de l'ancienne France* XII: *Province ecclésiastique de Lyon* pt. 3: *Diocèses de Langres et de Dijon* (Archives de la France monastique v. 45) (Ligugé: 1941), 177.

[87] Pierre Quarré, "Les Statues de la Vierge à l'Enfant des confins burgondo-champenois au début du XIVe siècle," *Gazette des beaux-arts* CX (6e période v. LXXI) (1968): 201-2; Josef Adolf Schmoll gen. Eisenwerth, "Die Madonnna von Bayel (Südchampagne) und ihre Schlüsselrolle für die lothringische Skulptur des frühen 14. Jahrhunderts," *Wiener Jahrbuch für Kunstgeschichte* XLVI/XLVII t. 2 (1993/94): 641-65 passim, Abb. 9; Dorothy Gillerman, *Enguerran de Marigny and the Church of Notre-Dame at Ecouis* (University Park, PA: 1994), 25, 32; *L'Art au temps des rois maudits, Philippe le Bel et ses fils 1285-1328*, exh. cat. Grand Palais (Paris: 1998). Based on Bautier, they identify the tomb as that of Guillaume de Mussy and use it to date related groups of sculptures much earlier than had previous authors.

[88] Lambert, 352-61, quoting Vignier BNF fr. 5994 fol. 270v; Barthélemy, *Voyage*, 108; Arnaud, 222-23 and pl. 2 (drawing); Salet, "Mussy," 329 ill.

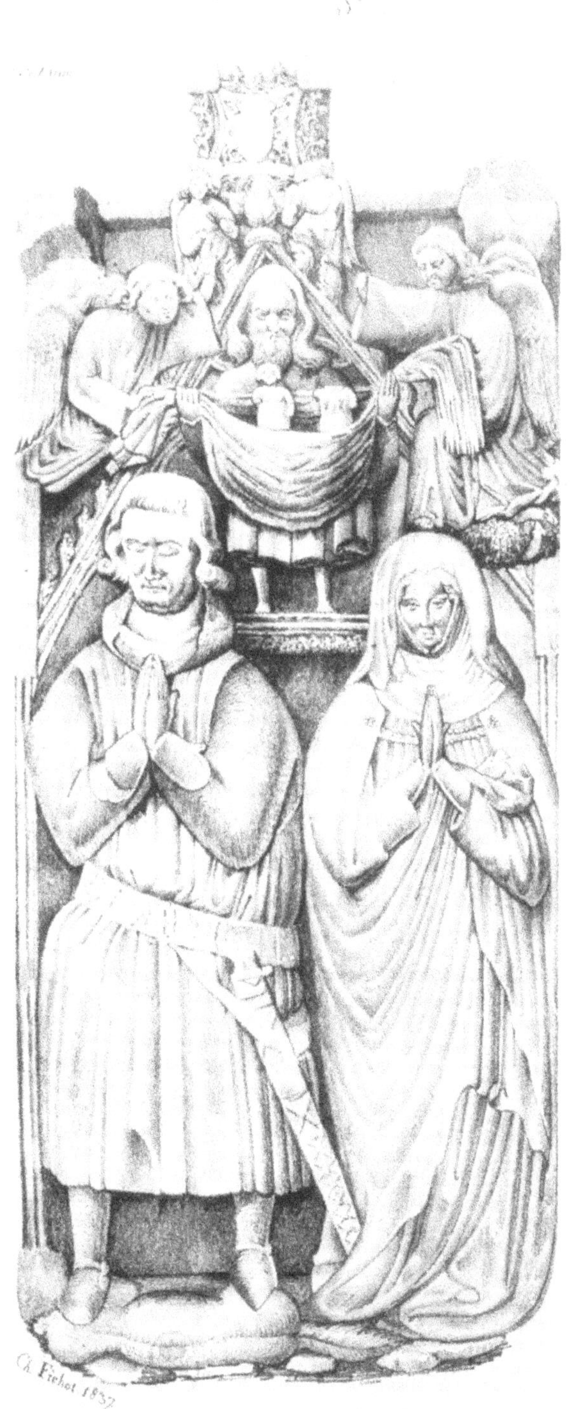

Fig. 33. Mussy. Tomb here identified as depicting Henri Caillot de Mussy (d. 1338) and his wife Jeannette. The stone at the top with effaced coat of arms was probably added by their son André (d. 1361) and is now lost. Drawing by Charles Fichot, 1837. (After Arnaud, 1837) (Photo: Paris, Bibliothèque nationale de France).

Gaignières tomb drawings, which have been published in approximate chronological order by Jean Adhémar.[89] The numbers below refer to illustrated entries in that publication.

The knight is bareheaded and his shoulder-length hair is cut in bangs at the forehead. He wears a coat of mail and a long sleeveless surcoat, with spurs, belt, harness and sword but—perhaps significantly—no shield. The long surcoat was in use ca. 1300 (no. 468, dated 1297; no. 480, of 1298), but retained in funerary art for a long time along with more up-to-date male fashions (see for example no. 811, of 1360). The wife wears a standard cloak with tie and a short head-veil that completely swathes her neck. Quicherat (1877) called such a head-covering a *touaille* and his example, a tomb of 1311,[90] has been used as proof of an early fourteenth-century date for the Mussy tomb. But the fashion Quicherat is describing always included 'horns' of hair above the ears. Béguines and nuns covered their heads as at Mussy through the fourteenth century, and the veiled neck had long connoted the older married woman. An illumination in the Maciejowski Bible (Pierpont Morgan M638 fol. 17r, before 1250) illustrates Ruth I:14-19, showing Naomi and her daughters-in-law, all widows. Only Naomi's head-covering hides her neck while the younger women's do not.[91] Such an 'mature woman's veil' lasts a very long time in tomb art; no. 760 (1349) and no. 779 (after 1352) are by no means the last examples in the Gaignières series, and one could also mention among examples of the upper nobility no. 846 (1371) and no. 851 (1372).

Other details of the Mussy tomb perhaps may prove more useful for dating. Over the gisants is an architectural canopy filled with a gauche image of Abraham holding their souls in a blanket (Fig. 33). While the soul-in-blanket motif is fairly standard in the tombs of religious,[92] it is uncommon in monuments for the laity—and the inclusion of Abraham is extremely rare. The soul-in-blanket motif does occur, however, in a cluster of examples of incised tomb slabs from the region of Champagne:

---

[89] Jean Adhémar, "Les Tombeaux de la collection Gaignières," *Gazette des beaux-arts* CXVI (6e période v. LXXXIV) (1974) pp. 11-192.

[90] Jules Quicherat, *Histoire du costume en France depuis les temps les plus reculés jusqu'à la fin du XVIIIe siècle*, 2nd ed. (Paris: 1877) pp. 189-90; Bautier p. 96.

[91] Sydney Cockerell, ed., *Old Testament Miniatures* (New York: 1969) pp. 90-91.

[92] An early example is Gaignières no. 402, the sumptuous copper tomb of Mathieu de Vendôme, abbot of Saint-Denis, d. 1286. The early date of Gaignières no. 7, tomb of Abbot Pierre of Saint-Bénigne de Dijon, d. 1132, can be discounted: see Wilhelm Schlink, *Zwischen Cluny und Clairvaux, Die Kathedrale von Langres* (Berlin: 1970) p. 123 n. 369 and Abb. 111.

no. 459 (Châlons-sur-Marne, 1296) with an earlier style of canopy than Mussy; no. 646 (1325, Simone d'Arceau, dame de Marac, buried at Saint-Pierre d'Arceau);[93] no. 737 (Châlons, 1334 and 1344). To these can be added the only example, other than Mussy, that I have found of a lay tomb with Abraham holding the blanket: no. 711 (Châlons), depicting three figures, the last of whom died in the same year as Henri Caillot de Mussy, 1338.[94] The Mussy tomb thus compares in iconography with a constricted regional group dated in the second quarter of the fourteenth century. It is more likely to be the tomb of Henri Caillot (d. 1338) than of Guillaume de Mussy (d. 1306/8), who in any event would probably have insisted on a much less mediocre, provincial example of the stone-carver's art.

Could Henri Caillot be called a founder of Mussy? A commemorative funerary slab made in 1361 upon the death of his son André, and now set into the west wall of the south transept, establishes that the father and mother had founded a chaplaincy at the altar of John the Baptist. The inscription, which has been transcribed frequently and variously, can be translated:[95]

> Here lies Sire Hanriz Quailloz de Muxi who died in the year 1338 and Jehanete his wife, who founded herein [in this church] a perpetual chaplaincy which provides 3 masses a week at the altar of St John the Baptist, and they gave 40 sous a year for 4 anniversaries, and between the burials of the two lies Andrez their son, who had founded a chaplaincy of 3 masses at the aforementioned altar and gave 60 sous a year for 3 anniversaries, and died in the year 1361, and they lie within [the tomb], the heir also. May they rest in peace (Requiem in pace).

No date can be established for the chaplaincy donation of Henri and Jeannette; their son André established his in 1348, thirteen years before his death.[96]

---

[93] For Marac see Fig. 1. Jean Marilier, "Les Tombes médiévales de l'église d'Arceau," *Mémoires de la Commission des antiquités du départment de la Côte-d'Or* XXXIV (1984-86) pp. 269-70, fig. 3. Her anniversary at Langres cathedral was founded by her uncle, the canon Jean d'Arceau: Roussel, *Le Diocèse de Langres* IV p. 79.

[94] See Didron (as in p. 31 n. 30 above), p. 287, ill. p. 282.

[95] For various readings of the inscription see Arnaud p. 223; Lambert p. 372; Bautier p. 96 n. 4; Salet, "Mussy" p. 336. The end of the inscription, following the date 1361, has proved most controversial, having been recorded most recently as "et gisent li hoirs aussi ceant. R.C.I.PAC." "Requiem in pace" makes the most sense here.

[96] Roserot, *Dictionnaire* II p. 1008. The earliest surviving record of a chaplaincy at that altar is a donation in 1300 by Perrenet Barottier and Jacquette his wife, from Ricey:

I would suggest that André—who was interred in his parents' tomb between their bodies—had the 1361 plaque added to, or perhaps substituted for, the original tomb inscription (if indeed it had one). And it was probably André who added the coat of arms at the top, seen by Vignier. Arnaud (1837) published the Fichot drawing of the founders' tomb including the added escutcheon (Fig. 33), which by then had been scraped illegible—vandalized in the Revolution, presumably—and he added that the stone on which the arms had been carved was a separate stone ("rapportée"), adding "Il est aisé de voir à l'ornement qui l'entoure qu'il est d'une époque postérieure au travail des statues" (it is easy to see from the ornament framing the shield that it is of a later period than the workmanship of the statues).[97]

Thus the stone with the de Mussy coat of arms was added to the tomb, probably by André. One is led inevitably to the conclusion that the coat of arms added to the tomb was mid fourteenth century, comparable to the vault keystone in the fourteenth-century nave, and part of a pattern of giving to the church established in Henri Caillot's branch of the family. Since Henri was of the generation of Guillaume de Mussy's sons Pierre and Jean, all of whom died in the 1330s-40s, it is unlikely that he himself was the kneeling knight represented in the stained glass ensemble of the choir of Mussy, ca. 1288-90. So who was he?

The "bande componée" and the Origin of the Arms de Mussy

I have tried to establish that there is no evidence whatsoever that the de Mussy family was armigerous when the church of Mussy was built and glazed in the late 1280s. Guillaume, the corrupt royal bailiff, sealed with the arms of the bishopric of Langres, seigneur of Mussy-sur-Seine. Examples of coats of arms firmly connected to the de Mussy family only appear later, in the third quarter of the fourteenth century. Before 1300 there is only the stained glass shield at Mussy. I propose that it is the only surviving element of the choir window seen by Vignier—a kneeling knight in a heraldic surcoat—and that that glass was a memorial to Guillaume's brother Gui, a soldier of Charles d'Anjou in 1278 and thus undoubtedly slain in the massacre of 30 March 1282 known as the Sicilian Vespers. Such a memorial would have been the gift of his family, or perhaps even the queen of Sicily. He was slaughtered while serving in her husband's forces, and she had been there—in Naples, not Sicily, or she

---

Lambert p. 364. They are discussed p. 76 below.

[97] Arnaud p. 225, pl. 2; Lambert p. 359 n. 1.

and Charles might have shared his fate. Petit has commented on the local reaction to this tragedy:[98]

> The news only reached France sometime later. That sympathy which accompanies misfortune seized a certain number of knights anxious to avenge the death of their brothers in arms....Charles d'Anjou had led off his *féodaux* of the Tonnerre region, families' younger sons whom he had bound to his service, and who would never return to their native land. Other lords of the province had joined this endeavor, and had been seeking in those distant lands a fortune and a situation that they couldn't find at home.

The later donations and important burials, in the church of Mussy, of Sire Henri Caillot and his son André—and the arms that André probably added to his father's tomb—further suggest that they were Gui's descendants. In the same generation as André, after 1350, another branch of the de Mussy family (probably descendants of Guillaume's son Jean) seem to have taken arms that they differenced from those in Gui's memorial.

One returns full circle to the question of the origin of the arms 'de Mussy'—that is, why would the soldier Gui have chosen the arms to be seen in the stained glass shield. The arms in the Mussy window (Fig. 28) are, let it be noted, odd in several respects. They incorporate an unusually large number of potential *brisures* (border, *bande*, *chef*); the *bande* and *chef* are not often found together, and when they are, the *bande* normally does not surmount the entire shield as at Mussy, but issues from below the *chef*.[99] Even stranger is the *bande componée*, extremely rare in thirteenth-century heraldry. Only one French family is recorded as having used it, and then only for their cadets (Trie, in the Oise).[100]

---

[98] Petit, *Histoire* VI pp. 39-41. The gift of a house to the bishop by Guillaume de Mussy in 1287 could be part of this theorized memorial project. The charter is published by Lambert pp. 537-38. I have taken it as potentially significant that the house (located *juxta pontem*, at the bridge) may have been the same one (*propè pontem*) later rented by the bishop to Henri Caillot (Lambert pp. 372-73), whom I have proposed as Gui de Mussy's son (see genealogical chart).

[99] Fox-Davies (as in p. 47 n. 58 above), pp. 113-14.

[100] The arms used by the cadets of Trie were *d'or à la bande componée d'argent et d'azur bordée de gueules*, the *bande componée* and *bordure* being derived from the family's county of Dammartin. The best explications of the Trie arms are by Max Prinet, "Armorial de France composé à la fin du XIIIe siècle ou au commencement du XIVe [Chifflet-Prinet Roll, now dated 1297]," *Le Moyen âge* XXXI (1920) pp. 11-12 nos. 25-26; Prinet, "Armoiries françaises et allemandes décrites dans un ancien rôle d'armes anglais [Walford's Roll]," *Le Moyen âge* XXXIV (1923) p. 249 no. 61. See also *Rolls of Arms* (as

There is, however, one famous coat of arms from Champagne with a prominent *bande componée*—or, counter-compony (*échiquetée*),[101] that is, with a double row of alternating compons instead of merely one. The arms of the Cistercian motherhouse of Clairvaux (Aube) are *de sable à la bande échiquetée* (= counter-compony) *d'argent et de gueules* (Fig. 34). These arms are commonly presumed to have been the arms of St Bernard's family of Fontaines-lez-Dijon,[102] though it is possible that they came to Clairvaux from the arms of the patron Hugues count of Troyes and Bar-sur-Aube (d. 1125). This at least was the considered opinion of Chifflet, after an examination of the (totally different) arms borne by Fontaines.[103]

---

in p. 40 n. 47 above) p. 194 no. 128 (Walford's Roll).

One Englishman used a *bande componée*: Sir John Mauleverer (*de gueules au chef d'or à la bande componée d'azur et argent*) in the Nativity Roll of 1306/8, court of Edward I. See Noel Denholm-Young, *History and Heraldry 1254 to 1310* (Oxford: 1965) pp. 117-18; Gerard Brault, *Eight Thirteenth-Century Rolls of Arms in French and Anglo-Norman Blazon* (University Park, Pa: 1973) pp. 11, 94 no. 18.

The *bande componée* noted by Pastoureau (maréchal Jean Clément du Metz, Chartres cathedral bay 116) is his error: Michel Pastoureau, "L'Armoirie médiévale: Une image théorique," in *Iconographie médiévale: Image, texte, contexte*, ed.Gaston Duchet-Sucheaux (Paris: 1990). The *bande* at Chartres is *gueules*; see the color plate in Jean Villette, *Les Vitraux de Chartres* (Rennes: 1979) p. 156.

[101] The term "contra-componé" in French heraldry has an extremely specific usage not applicable here: see glossary of Johannes Baptist Rietstap, *Armorial général* I (1884, rpt. London: 1965) p. xviii. See pp. xx-xxi for his entry for *échiqueté*, which clearly specifies that two rows of compons are normal for a *bande échiquetée*; when it has more than two they must be specified. In English heraldry, two rows are counter-compony and three or more are chequy: for an illustration see Fox-Davies p. 140 (applied to borders) and pp. 111-12 (discussion of bend compony and bend chequy).

[102] See for example Marie-Anselme Dimier and Maur Cocheril, "Quelques blasons d'abbayes cisterciennes de l'ancien diocèse de Langres," *Mémoires de la Société historique et archéologique de Langres* V (1961) p. 84. I am most grateful to Pierre-Gilles Girault for advice on the Clairvaux arms. While the oldest known examples are fifteenth century, he notes the thirteenth-century sculpted arms of Cistercian Noirlac (Cher): Girault, "Les Armoiries des abbayes de Noirlac et de Selles: à propos d'un sceau inédit," in *Mélanges Jean-Yves Ribault, Cahiers d'archéologie et d'histoire du Berry*, hors-série (Bourges 1996) pp. 161-67.

[103] Pierre-François Chifflet, *Sancti Bernardi Clarevallensis abbatis genus illustre assertum* (1660), reprinted Migne, *Patrologia latina* v. 185 pt. 2 (Paris: 1854) cols. 1533-35. On Hugues see Theodore Evergates, *Feudal Society in the Bailliage of Troyes under the Counts of Champagne, 1152-1284* (Baltimore: 1975) p. 2. He was a cadet of the house of Blois/Champagne and when he died childless his lands transferred back to his nephew Thibaut II (d. 1152), father of Henri the Liberal, count of Champagne (d. 1181). While Hugues' arms cannot be established, those of Blois/Champagne always used a decorated

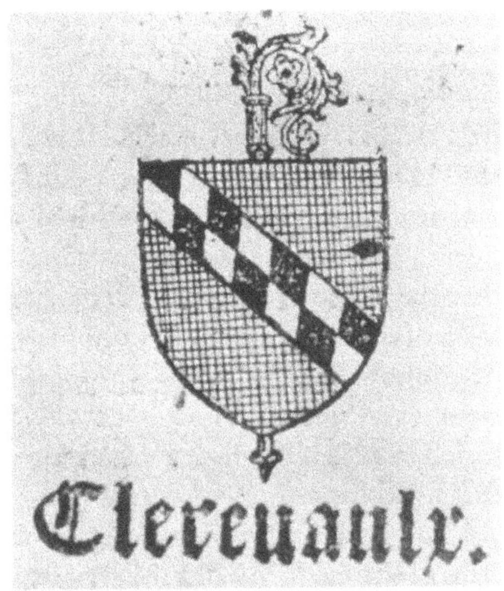

Fig. 34. Arms of Clairvaux: *de sable à la bande échiquetée d'argent et de gueules*. Troyes, Bibliothèque de la ville. (After Watkin Williams, *Studies in St. Bernard of Clairvaux*, 1927)

The arms in the choir window of Mussy not only add both a border and a *chef* but also reverse the tinctures of Clairvaux, using *gueules* for the field and *sable* for the compons that alternate with those in *argent*. The simplification of the *bande* (from counter-compony to compony) may be no more than the glazier's solution to the challenge of this extremely rare, complicated, and—through the expansion of the Cistercian order—world famous heraldry.

The connection of the de Mussy family to Clairvaux was cordial over at least four generations. They appear in the Clairvaux cartulary as early as 1147, and in every successive generation before that of Guillaume and his brothers. In 1213 their grandfather Guiard Pignot (Viardus Pignaus), *châtelain* of Mussy for the bishop of Langres and a donor to Clairvaux, was chosen as arbiter of a dispute between Clairvaux and the abbey of Pothières.[104] The father of Guillaume de Mussy—and of his soldier brother Gui—died when both were children, while their grandfather, a man of great local importance, may still have been alive (see chart Fig. 29). Guillaume, in sealing with the arms of the bishops of Langres, and Gui, basing his arms in the field of battle on those of Clairvaux, consciously or unconsciously may have been honoring the memory of their grandfather.

---

bande: see discussion in *Rolls of Arms* pp. 164-66.

[104] Bautier pp. 66-67 and his genealogical chart; Lambert p. 176. Garnier de Mussy, probably Gui's uncle, appears in the Clairvaux cartulary and may have had a son named Bernard.

Summation and Addendum

This chapter, which is entitled "What Ornament and Heraldry Reveal," has searched the stained glass ensemble remaining at Mussy for clues to its agenda. The ornament—grisaille, border design, canopywork—was analyzed in style and compared with other French Gothic monuments. The exercise provided a dating around 1285-90, somewhat earlier than the period to which Mussy has been assigned previously. Consideration of the unique marguerite borders (Fig. 10) and the fragments of an inscription (Fig. 28) led to a proposed connection with Marguerite de Bourgogne, queen of Sicily, newly widowed and returned to her native region in 1285. The firm evidence encoded in heraldry elaborated upon that hypothesis.

Of the three surviving coats of arms in the windows, one presents the arms of Vienne (Fig. 22), a regional family related by marriage to Bishop Gui de Genève (d. 1291), while another depicts the arms of Rochefort (Fig. 25), family of the canon who served as the chapter's treasurer and would be elected Bishop Gui's successor in 1296. The third coat of arms (Fig. 28), traditionally and erroneously attributed to Guillaume de Mussy, is the most atypical in its heraldry—as well as the most complicated from a genealogical perspective. The "Mussy arms" (Fig. 28) were compared to other examples of the same heraldry in the church, mostly now lost: an overpainted nave keystone (Fig. 6 no. 5), a lost window depicting a knight in heraldic surcoat, and the effaced shield once adorning the surviving 'founder's tomb' (Fig. 33). Related but somewhat different arms adorned many late medieval objects in the nearby church at Chaource (Fig. 30), and an investigation into that branch of the family de Mussy established its probable lineage through Guillaume de Mussy's son Jean (d. between 1347-52). This hypothesis appears on the genealogical chart Fig. 29.

My conclusion is that the "Mussy arms" (Fig. 28) probably were used by Guillaume de Mussy's brother Gui in his military career in the field with Charles d'Anjou in southern Italy, where he undoubtedly was massacred in 1282. The lost window at Mussy was, I believe, a memorial to him, and the 'founder's tomb' (Fig. 33), I have tried to establish, was the burial locus of his line—Henri Caillot (d. 1338) and his wife and son. Thus the church of Mussy in the fourteenth century was "their" church just as Chaource was the favored church of the other branch of the family, descended from Guillaume de Mussy through his son Jean.

Finally I have assayed an explanation for the eccentric choice of arms by the soldier Gui de Mussy. Through tinctures and its rare *bande componée*, his heraldry can be related to the Cistercian abbey of Clairvaux in the diocese of Langres (Fig. 34), the famous monastery that his grandfather had served in important lay functions. Certainly Clairvaux was associated with his homeland and with his family, but it is worth noting that Charles d'Anjou founded two Cistercian abbeys in southern Italy in the 1270s.

Charles's two Cistercian foundations, coeval, were built by French masons and occupied by French monks. Santa Maria della Vittoria (Abruzzi), founded 1274 and consecrated 1278, commemorated his victory over Conradin (1268) and was sited on the battlefield of Tagliacozzo.[105] Realvalle, near Mount Vesuvius, was begun the same year and occupied in 1279 by thirty-seven monks arriving from Royaumont. It commemorated Charles's defeat of Manfred in the battle of Benevento (1266).[106] In southern Italy in the 1270s, Gui de Mussy's choice of arms derived from the tinctures and *bande* of Clairvaux—and loaded with *brisures* denoting dependence and cadency—would have made a powerful personal talisman for a soldier in combat.

---

[105] Charles was imitating his grandfather Philippe Auguste who built Notre-Dame de la Victoire to commemorate the battle of Bouvines: Robert Branner, *St Louis and the Court Style in Gothic Architecture* (London: 1965) pp. 134-35. S. Maria della Vittoria was vaulted by 1282; an earthquake destroyed it ca. 1502 and in 1550 the site was abandoned. See bibliography in Caroline Bruzelius, "ad modum franciae. Charles of Anjou and Gothic Architecture in the Kingdom of Sicily," *Journal of the Society of Architectural Historians* 50 (1991) pp. 402-20, esp. 402 n. 2, figs. 1-3, 13.

[106] Realvalle was closed in 1805; in modern times the conversi wing has been occupied by a children's center. See Bruzelius, passim, esp. p. 402 n. 2, figs. 4, 5, 11, 12.

PART III

THE HOSPITAL OF TONNERRE AND THE QUEEN OF SICILY

The Capetian princess Marguerite de Bourgogne (ca. 1249-1308), widow of Charles d'Anjou, carved her niche in history by the foundation and construction of the hospital of Tonnerre (Figs. 35, 36), part of which survives, and her retirement there to serve its suffering population. Granddaughter of the great Burgundian duke Hugues IV and niece of Duke Robert II (ruled 1272-1306), as queen she was at times entrusted with the stewardship of her husband's realm and ran a brilliant Neapolitan court with a household of nearly 300 for which the records of luxurious consumption remain.[1] Her father died at Acre in 1266, her mother (a Bourbon) even earlier. All Marguerite's formative years were passed at the abbey of Fontevrault where her great-great-grandmother Mahaud de Courtenay (d. 1257) was retired. In October 1268 she became the second wife of Charles d'Anjou (1220-85), brother of St Louis and king of Sicily. It was a tumultuous time to live in southern Italy, a time which—may one be forgiven for saying—gave a different slant to the Italian adage *Vedere Napoli, poi mori* (See Naples and die). Within weeks of her wedding her new husband put to death Conradin; in 1270 the crusade of St Louis came to a dismal end in Tunis; in 1276 Charles

---

[1] Robert Luyt, *La Princesse charitable et aulmoniere, ou l'histoire de la reyne Marguerite de Bourgongne, comtesse de Tonnerre ...* (Troyes: 1653, rpt. Tonnerre: 1979); Anselme I pp. 397, 544; Louis Le Maistre, "Marguerite de Bourgogne, reine de Naples, de Sicile et de Jérusalem, comtesse de Tonnerre," *Annuaire historique du département de l'Yonne* (1867) pp. 43-109; Gaston Sirjean, *Encyclopédie généalogique des maisons souveraines du monde, Branches cadettes* IX (I no. 9), *Première maison de Bourgogne* (Paris: 1964) p. 20; Jean Richard, "Marguerite de Bourgogne, reine de Jérusalem," *Actes du VIIe centenaire de l'Hôtel-Dieu des Fontenilles, Tonnerre 1292-1992*, ed. Line Skórka and Jean-Pierre Fontaine, *Bulletin annuel de la Société d'archéologie et d'histoire du Tonnerrois*, no. 45 supplément (1992) pp. 21-33. On her household: Georges Lemoine, "La Maison et les toilettes de Marguerite de Bourgogne," *Bulletin de la Société des sciences historiques et naturelles de l'Yonne* LXXV (série 5 v. V)(1921) pp. 43-50, reprinting Paul Durrieu, *Les Archives angevines de Naples, étude sur les registres du roi Charles Ier (1265-1285)* I (Paris: 1886) pp. 65-66, 129-32.

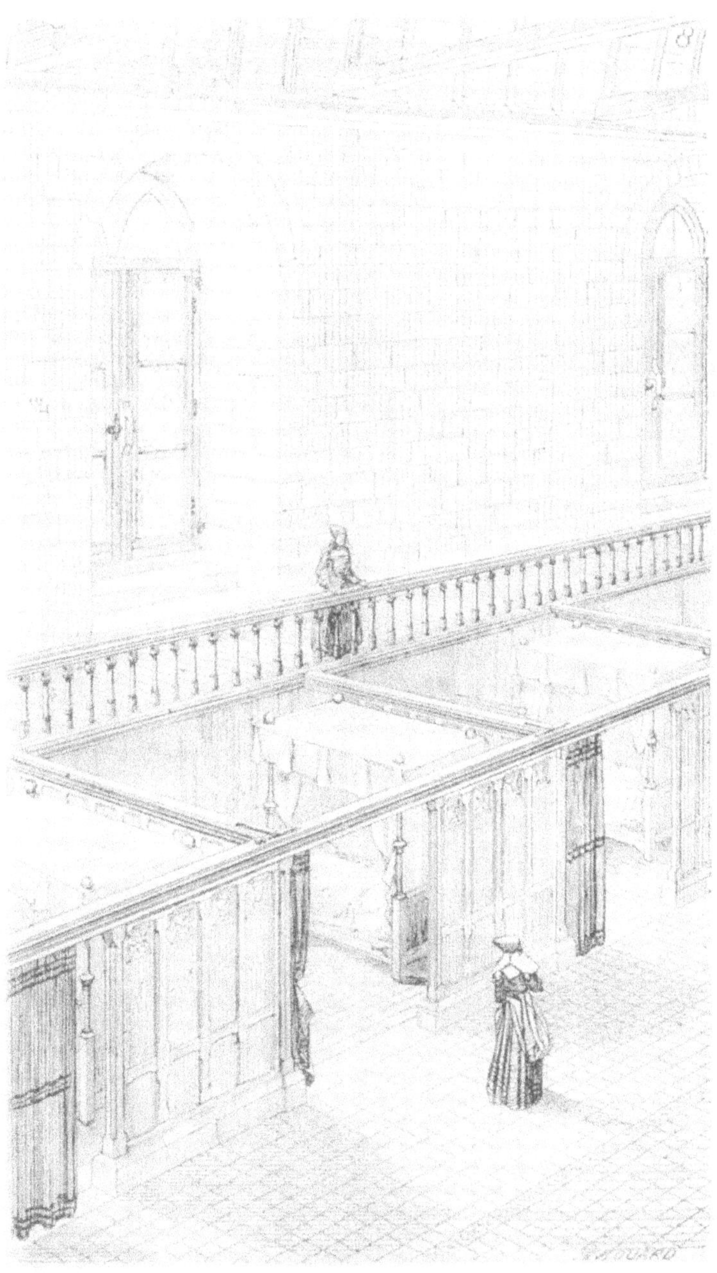

Fig. 35. Tonnerre (Yonne), Hôtel-Dieu de Notre-Dame des Fontenilles. Ca. 1293-95. Reconstruction of interior. (After Viollet-le-duc, 1868)

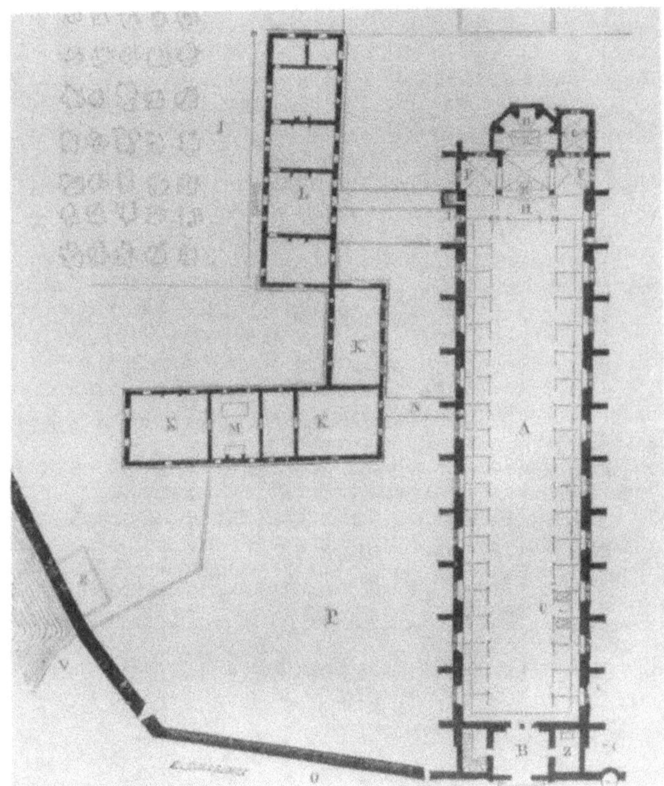

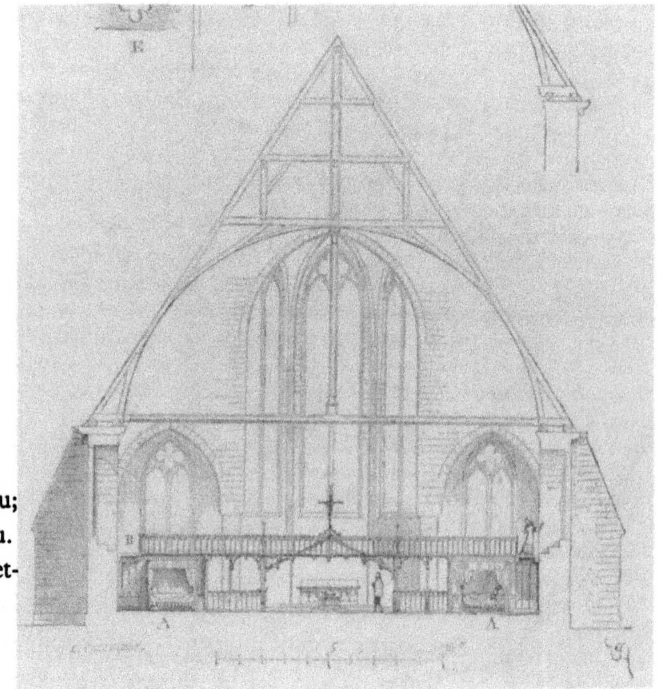

Fig. 36. Tonnerre. Plan of Hôtel-Dieu and château; and section of Hôtel-Dieu. Ca. 1293-95. (After Viollet-le-duc, 1868)

received the heady but empty title of king of Jerusalem, for which he made plans to fight; in 1282 his troops were massacred at the Sicilian Vespers; in 1284 in Naples the capture and imprisonment by the admiral Roger de Lauria of Charles' son and heir. Charles himself died at the beginning of 1285 and Marguerite, leaving Naples in the hands of Robert d'Artois, returned to Paris with the heart of her husband for deposit at the Jacobins.

She had returned to her county of Tonnerre by May of 1285[2] and spent the next year or so putting her affairs in order with her inheritance and with her uncle, the duke (Petit p. 55, nos. 4705, 4762, 4805-8, 4812). By 1286 Marguerite had begun her religious benefactions. In November she founded a chaplaincy at the Cistercian nunnery of La Charité-lès-Lézinnes (Yonne), where she also established her anniversary (Petit p. 84, nos. 4772-73, 4863, 4876). The following year she negotiated various benefices with the Cistercian abbey of Fontenay (nos. 4804, 4833); as countess of Tonnerre she was hereditary defender of Cistercian Pontigny, and many documents of the late 1280s established her close interest in that abbey.[3] In July of 1289 one of the many privileges accorded Marguerite by Pope Nicholas IV was the right of entry to Cistercian abbeys with eight companions three times a year (provided she neither dined nor slept there; no. 5857). By 1288 she had begun buying land (nos. 4717, 4875, 4879, 4880, 4890, 4893-94, 4949); other purchases appear in the cartulary of theTonnerre hospital, but there is nothing to suggest that she had formulated that life-work explicitly by 1288.[4] At the end of 1290 she exchanged her dower rights in Anjou for a pension (life-rent *en viagère*).[5] By then she was certainly constructing three chapels at her château of

---

[2] Petit, *Histoire* VI, *pièce justificative* no. 4700. For simplicity's sake the data in this paragraph are accompanied by Petit numbers, though many of the charters are also available elsewhere.

[3] A will she may have made when pregnant in 1272 included donations to Cîteaux and Pontigny: Le Maistre (1867) pp. 58, 103.

[4] Ernest Petit, "Archives de l'hôpital de Tonnerre. Le cartulaire. L'obituaire," *Bulletin historique et philologique du Comité des travaux historiques et scientifiques* (1906) p. 19 (fol. 206), p. 20 (fol. 229), pp. 21-22 (fols. 306v-307r, purchases made from Gaucher de Rochefort, brother of Jean de Rochefort). Jean was at that time treasurer of the chapter of Langres (see at p. 45 n. 55 above).

[5] Armand Bellée, "Les Revenus d'une reine au XIIIe siècle, à propos d'un fait inédit de l'histoire du Maine," *Bulletin de la Société d'agriculture, sciences et arts de la Sarthe* XIX (série 2 v. XI) (1867-68) pp. 838-56.

Maulne, dedicated to saints Mary, Margaret and Catherine, for the repose of her husband's soul.[6] Papal documents attest to their completion and staffing by chaplains before August 1291 (nos. 5908-9). The pontiff refers to her heavy expenses to repair her various châteaux as well as to put her financial house in order (no. 5911).

It is only in mid 1292 that there is any definite indication that Marguerite had made the decision to build the hospital and retire there from the world: in July she gave her château of Brugny (Marne) to the duke (nos. 5074, 5111). The following January she settled her remaining estates on her nephews and heirs Robert de Flanders and Guillaume de Chalon, for a cash settlement plus a pension from each of them, and retention of the title of countess of Tonnerre during her lifetime.[7] She issued the momentous charter establishing the Hôtel-Dieu de Tonnerre during the Octave of Easter 1293.

Once the idea of the hospital had seized her imagination, all her thoughts and resources were directed there.[8] Thus it seems clear that any donation by Marguerite de Bourgogne to Mussy-sur-Seine would have been made before 1292. Indeed, the close similarity of the architectural style of Mussy and Tonnerre, as well as of their stained glass, to be discussed below, suggests that she found her craftsmen while they were working for the bishop of Langres.

What then were the ties between Tonnerre, Mussy, and Langres that could explain such an encounter? Tonnerre and Mussy, about fifty kilometers east, were on the *grand chemin tonnerrois* running west from Langres to Auxerre. Mussy was in the county of Tonnerre, and both Mussy and Tonnerre were in the diocese of Langres. As count and countess of Tonnerre, Marguerite and her husband had done homage to Bishop Gui de Genève for the county in 1274 (Petit nos. 4170, 4194, 4270), and she renewed that homage soon after her return to France as a

---

[6] Mathieu p. 121. She built hospices at Ligny and at Laignes, and a chapel at Augy, at unknown dates: Mathieu p. 124; Petit, *Histoire* VI pp. 195-96; Jean Fromageot, "La Figure, l'oeuvre et le souvenir de Marguerite de Bourgogne dans le Tonnerrois," *Bulletin annuel de la Société d'archéologie et d'histoire de Tonnerre* no. 26 (1973) p. 47. I would like to thank Terryl Kinder for obtaining the last reference for me.

[7] Robert got her far-flung *terres* in western France, Montmirail (Sarthe) and Alluye (Eure-et-Loir), and Guillaume got the county of Tonnerre and lands in the Berry: Le Maistre (1867) pp. 71-72.

[8] Only one later charter indicates another project: in 1297 she built a chapel in her château of Ligny (Petit, *Histoire* VI no. 5936).

widow (nos. 4750, 4809).

Upon her arrival on French soil in 1285 Marguerite would have been unable to avoid an increasingly unpleasant confrontation that was developing between the bishop of Langres and the Benedictine abbey of Pothières some seven kilometers south of Mussy (Côte-d'Or, arr. Châtillon).[9] Since 1153 Mussy had been divided between three *seigneurs*: the bishop, the abbot of Pothières, and the duke of Burgundy.[10] Clearly the peace between them was never easy, as attested by a succession of treaties through the next century. In 1245 an agreement reduced the role of the duke to *garde* of Pothières. In 1247 this right as defender was held by his son the count of Nevers, who was Queen Marguerite's father; by the 1270s she and her husband held the *garde* of Pothières, though their absence from France made for a difficult situation should any policing actually become necessary. Eventually, when it did, the duke and even the king's sergeant were called upon to fill in.[11]

Since 1207 the monks of Pothières had been exempted by the pope from the authority of the bishops of Langres, though whether this was a cause or an effect of their increasingly hostile and violent relationship is unclear. The arrogant personality and outrageous conduct of the abbot Pierre may have been central to the oncoming crisis, since already in 1284 his own monks had revolted against him with violence and vandalism.[12] The culminating incident involving Mussy occurred in the summer of 1288 (by which time Marguerite was well installed in her county), while Bishop Gui was in residence at his château at Mussy. A band of his agents joined by bourgeois of the town sought out Abbot Pierre in residence at one of his properties, which they pillaged, vandalized and burned, then proceeding to Pothières to rough up the monks. The bailiff of Mussy, a

---

[9] Pothières (Poulthiers, Pultariae): Cottineau (as in p. 19 n. 6) col. 2349. A useful overview of the conflict is in Belotte (as in p. 14 n. 21) pp. 186-87.

[10] Roserot, *Dictionnaire* II p. 1009; the accord was sealed by no less an eminence than St Bernard.

[11] The 1240s: Lambert pp. 7, 96, 527. The 1270s: Mathieu p. 116; Le Maistre (1867) pp. 56, 102; Petit, *Histoire* VI nos. 4650, 4724, p. 153 note (bull of 18 Dec. 1285). In 1269 Pothières had agreed with the bishop of Langres to exchange all its *biens* held in Mussy for revenues elsewhere: Lambert pp. 174, 535-36.

[12] The papal exemption: Maxime de Montrond, *Dictionnaire des abbayes et monastères* (Paris: 1856) col. 646. On the monks' revolt: Maurice Prou, "Additions et corrections au *Gallia christiana* tirées des registres d'Honorius IV," *Mélanges d'archéologie et d'histoire*, Ecole française de Rome, V (1885) pp. 261-62.

man called Guillaume Pou Villain, threatened the abbot with a pun on his name, "que il li abatroit sadite maison seur la teste, et que il sauroit se sa teste estoit aussi dure comme la pierre" (that he'd bring down his house on his head and he'd see if his head was as hard as rock).[13]

It is established that Marguerite's talents at peacemaking and reconciliation were recognized and used by her own squabbling family,[14] and one may suppose that as *garde* of Pothières in 1288 she did her very best to restore order, to succor the abbey, and to appease the grievances of the bishop of Langres. I suggest that that is the occasion and date of her donation to Mussy, which stylistic evidence suggests was just under construction at that moment.

The Hôtel-Dieu of Tonnerre

Queen Marguerite issued the elaborate foundation charter of the Hôpital Notre-Dame des Fontenilles de Tonnerre at Eastertide 1293, in which she laid out its organization and administration, its staffing, its revenues, and most impressively its *raison d'être*: following Matthew XXV: 35-46, to feed the hungry, give drink to the thirsty, take in strangers and pilgrims, clothe the naked, succor the sick, console prisoners, and bury the dead.[15] Again the foundation was for the repose of the soul of Charles d'Anjou, who appears in the hospital's *obituaire* as "fondator noster."[16] The immense structure, called by Salet "le plus beau témoin que la France possède de l'architecture hospitalière du Moyen Age," was completed and consecrated on 16 March 1295. The queen then

[13] The pun has not been recognized heretofore. The abbot complained to Parlement, an investigation was made, and the Mussy marauders—hearing that the king's agents were coming to Mussy to arrest them—fortified the bishop's château and destroyed bridges and trees to impede their approach. Abbot Pierre died probably by 1290 and Bishop Gui during the winter of 1290/91. The royal judgment of January 1292 ordered the bishop's bailiff and provost and the bourgeois to fully compensate Pothières (and the crown). Petit, *Histoire* VI pp. 151-54.

[14] Mathieu p. 124; Richard, *Les Ducs de Bourgogne* (as in p. 40 n. 48) pp. 322-23.

[15] The foundation charter is discussed and illustrated in Noël Quénée, *L'Hôpital Notre Dame des Fontenilles à Tonnerre*, 2nd ed. (La Pierre-qui-Vire: 1979) pp. 7-8, fig. 44.

[16] Petit, "Archives" p. 24. The execution of Conradin so close to their wedding has been suggested as the impetus for her charities in her husband's memory. In the same obituary Marguerite appears as "mater nostra, serventissima fondatrix istius Hospitalis" (p. 29).

built for her own use a château just to the north (destroyed ca. 1850), which was linked to the great hospital by a passageway. Except for raising of the floor in 1619 some forty to fifty centimeters, and 1763-67 truncations of the entrance area, the great hall of her hospital survives (Figs. 35, 36): almost 100 meters in length, over eighteen meters wide, the famous carpentry roof nearly matching that span in height.

The Architect of Mussy and Tonnerre?

Salet, in analyzing the architecture of Mussy and Tonnerre, came to the conclusion that both were designs by the same architect. Beyond a comparable clean-lined economy of form, without moldings or capitals, he noted such details as chamfered arches, rectangular *doubleaux*, and ribs 'dying' into their responds in a point (Figs. 3-4, 35, 51-52). Most unique at both sites is a double-wall extension outward at the base of the polygonal apse (Figs. 36, 50), flat-roofed and lit by small rectangular lights.[17] Following Lefèvre-Pontalis, Salet connected this designer with the name of Maître Geoffroy, mentioned in a 1297 document as living in Mussy when he received payment for visiting the chantier of Troyes cathedral to provide an architectural expertise. Thus Geoffroy was proposed as the architect of Mussy, and the 1297 date has subsequently dictated current scholarly opinion dating Mussy ca. 1296.[18]

But Tonnerre is firmly dated 1293-95 by charters, and the Mussy choir—according to the evidence amassed in this study—dates before 1292, probably to 1288-90. While I cannot offer a *curriculum vitae* for Maître Geoffroy, about whose work nothing is known, I can denote a stonemason connected with both projects, Mussy and Tonnerre. In the

---

[17] At Mussy this double-wall extension forms an exterior 'service corridor' around the apse, a totally unique feature. See Salet, "Mussy" pp. 325, 328, 330; Salet, "Tonnerre," p. 233. On such unsculpted detailing in England see Bony (as in p. 2 n. 3); Virginia Jansen, "Dying Mouldings, Unarticulated Springer Blocks, and Hollow Chamfers in Thirteenth-Century Architecture," *Journal of the British Archaeological Association* CXXXV (1982) pp. 35-54.

[18] Eugène Lefèvre-Pontalis, "L'Architecture gothique dans la Champagne méridionale au XIIIe et au XVIe siècle," *Congrès archéologique* LXIX (1902) p. 306, citing Fabric Accounts of Troyes (Paris, BNF MS lat. 9111, fol. 214v). For the dating of Mussy to ca. 1296 or later, see recently *L'Art au temps des rois maudits* (as in p. 58 n. 87 above) pp. 36, 114, 377.

Tonnerre obituary is an entry "obiit Jaqueta, uxor Perinete *lathomi*, et dictus Perinetus nobis legavit III francos aureos."[19] I propose to identify them with the couple who on 26 March 1300 founded one of the first chaplaincies at Mussy: Perrenet Barottier and Jacquette his wife, living at Ricey (see Fig. 1), the location of their gift of revenues.[20] Barottier is a sobriquet: *barattier* = knavish, roguish, rascally.[21]

Furthermore, I believe that a reasonable case can be made to identify the rascally Perrenet and his wife with the kneeling bourgeois couple whose images are now in Mussy Bay 102 (Fig. 14). While they are anonymous, without inscription, perhaps they were not always without identifying 'heraldry.' In Fichot's watercolor of 1840 (Fig. 6 no. 3) is a shield that he saw in the choir windows but which did not survive Didron's restoration. It is difficult to blazon since the charge in *chef* is irregular. One might say: *d'argent à une fasce d'or accompagnée en chef d'un chevron renversé de gueules.* Note first that the arms are *à enquerre*, metal on metal (contrary to the rules of heraldry); such arms are extremely rare and usually quite provincial.[22] What can one say about the reversed chevron, or whatever it is?

One possibility would be that it is a glazier's simplification of a *dance* (*fasce vivrée*). There is one family in the region that bore arms with a *fasce* accompanied by a *dance* in *chef*, in variations of these tinctures—Sergines, from the vicinity of Sens. While they served Charles d'Anjou in Naples,[23] nothing connects them with southern Champagne or with Mussy.

---

[19] Petit, "Archives" p. 29 (August, Octave of the Assumption).

[20] Lambert p. 364.

[21] *Baretiere* is used in this sense by Jean de Meung, author of the continuation of Roman de la Rose (born in the Berry ca. 1250, d. by 1305). For other examples see: Jean-Baptiste de La Curne de Sainte-Palaye, *Dictionnaire historique de l'ancien langage françois* I (Niort: 1875-82) p. 395; Frédéric Godefroy, *Dictionnaire de l'ancienne langue française* I (Paris: 1881) pp. 577-78.

[22] Fox-Davies (as in p. 47 n. 58) pp. 74, 85; Rietstap (as in p. 64 n. 101) I p. xxi.

[23] The arms of Sergines: Coulon p. 83 no. 482 (1288); Douët-d'Arcq no. 11806; *Rolls of Arms* 201 (Walford's Roll no. 175); Prinet, "Armoiries françaises" pp. 251-52 no. 67 (Walford's Roll); Paul Adam-Even and Léon Jéquier, "Un Armorial français du XIIIe siècle, L'armorial Wijnberghen," *Archives héraldiques suisses, Annuaire* LXVIII (1954) p. 59 (no. 857), p. 68 (no. 1118). On the service of the Sergines family in Naples see Durrieu II p. 378.

There is another possibility. If what Fichot saw was a coat of arms with, in *chef*, a mason's square or compass, the *fasce* might be a mason's rule or level[24]—and the following hypothesis might be suggested. According to my reconstruction of the original program, which appears at the conclusion of this study, the most likely place for this lost Fichot shield would be Bay 4, while the clerestory Bay 104 above probably held the bourgeois couple (see pp. 102, 111 below). If the couple in Fig. 14 represents the mason Perrenet Barottier and his wife Jacquette, who in 1300 established a chaplaincy at Mussy, and who are recorded in an obit at Tonnerre, the bizarre arms in the lost shield would be extremely logical— not only the 'reversed chevron' but also the *à enquerre* tinctures, since they would be arms invented by a rich craftsman without heraldic ancestry.

It has already been suggested that the grisailles of Mussy and Tonnerre, like the architecture, share a similar stylistic affinity. In order to establish the extent of their kinship, one needs to know a great deal more about both ensembles.

The Queen's Diamond Necklace

The vast ensemble of stained glass of the Hôtel-Dieu of Tonnerre can now be conjured up only in the mind's eye.[25] It is a sad undertaking to recount the slings and arrows of its outrageous fortune. Less than thirty damaged panels and fragments survive, making poignantly clear the magnitude of our loss. The great hall originally had some twenty bays along the flanks, each containing twenty-four grisaille panels (including the curved lancet heads) arranged in six rows across a pair of lancets. The polygonal apse was more elegantly lit by five doublet bays of extraordinary height headed by quatrefoil traceries, and its flanking chapels each contained two shorter bays of the same doublet-and-rose fenestra-

---

[24] On mason's tools: Bernard George Morgan, *Canonic Design in English Medieval Architecture* (Liverpool: 1961); Lon Shelby, "Medieval Masons' Tools: The Level and the Plumb Rule," *Technology and Culture* II (1961) pp. 127-30; Shelby, "Medieval Masons' Tools II: Compass and Square," *Technology and Culture* VI (1965) esp. pp. 242, 245.

[25] Viollet-le-duc's reconstruction drawing (my Fig. 35) shows the bays of the great hall inaccurately, and his statement that colored glass filled the polygonal sanctuary is without foundation: Eugène Viollet-le-duc, *Dictionnaire raisonné de l'architecture française* VI (Paris: 1868) p. 112.

tion. In all there were nine tracery heads filled with colored glass in the eastern chapels, and well over 600 bulged-quarry grisailles altogether. Bombing in 1940 further destroyed the few panels that had been salvaged in the nineteenth century, after massive damage probably when the baroque altar was installed as well as vandalism at the French Revolution, when the queen's tomb also disappeared.[26]

The glass of Tonnerre was mentioned in passing in 1653 by Robert Luyt in his biography of the queen:[27]

> Il y à une preuve visible [of her love for her husband] ... dans toutes les fenestres de ce beau Temple, où l'on voit par tout l'image de Charles son mary & ses armes, lesquelles cette bonne Reine fit mettre aupres des siennes dans les lozanges qui sont opposées l'une a l'autre.
> (There is visible proof of her love for her husband in all the windows of this beautiful temple, where can be seen everywhere the image of her husband Charles and his arms, which this good queen had placed near hers in lozenges opposite one another.)

Dormois, in 1852, states without reference that the windows had been broken in 1793, noting that two north bays still contained some old grisailles and that some of the apsidal traceries kept their colored glass, each bay of a different design. Baron de Guilhermy, a visitor to Tonnerre two years later, also recorded colored glass *à rinceaux* in the tracery lights of the chapel, and enumerated the grisaille panels within colored borders surviving in the two north windows.[28] In the first one, the lozenges at the centers of the grisaille panels displayed three heads of kings, three of queens, and three each of their coats of arms, while in the second window

---

[26] The tall bays of the apse were blinded at the bottom, probably when the baroque altar now blocking them was installed. For good illustrations see Quénée figs. 2, 8, 9. On the queen's tomb see p. 112 n. 21 below.

[27] Luyt (as in p. 68 n. 1 above) p. 43. Luyt's witness refutes the recent assertion that the Tonnerre glass may have included other coats of arms now lost, and thus that some of the crowned heads did not depict Marguerite or Charles d'Anjou: *L'Art au temps des rois maudits* p. 387.

[28] Camille Dormois, "Description des bâtiments de l'hôpital de Tonnerre," *Bulletin de la Société des sciences historiques et naturelles de l'Yonne* VI (1852) p. 179; François de Guilhermy, "Notes sur diverses localités de la France," Paris, BNF N. Acq. fr. 6110 fols. 34v-35r (1854). See also Maximilien Quantin, *Répertoire archéologique du département de l'Yonne* (Paris: 1868) col. 275. Several nineteenth-century photos in the Bibliothèque du Patrimoine, Paris, show these glass fragments.

Fig. 37. Tonnerre. Drawing by Boeswillwald of panels restored in 1880. (Photo: Paris, Arch. phot.)

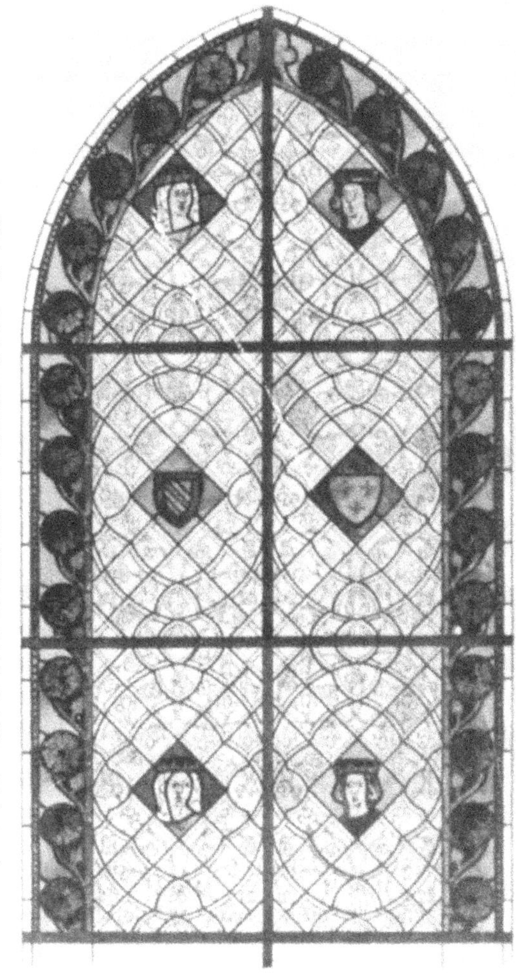

there were two lozenges of each of these four elements—making a total of twenty surviving panels of grisaille.

An 1880 drawing by the architect Boeswillwald (Fig. 37) gives some idea of the general appearance of these bays, though neither it nor the Socard drawing of 1913 (Fig. 38) renders the grisaille pattern with complete accuracy.[29] Each of the paired lancets had a central vertical iron, allowing for two grisaille panels side by side in each lancet, a left panel

[29] The restoration for which the Boeswillwald *devis* was submitted never took place according to Salet, "Tonnerre" p. 227. The Socard drawing was published in Paul Biver and Edmond Socard, "Le Vitrail civil au XIVe siècle," *Bulletin monumental* LXXVII (1913) p. 259.

with central lozenge of the queen's head facing one with the king on the right, and lozenges with their coats of arms in panels below. Rows of heads and rows of shields alternated to fill the lancet.

A restoration of 1907 seems to have rearranged the survivors further.[30] The fragments that remained following the 1940 bombing, which hit the north flank, were placed in storage until 1974, when photos and a preliminary inventory were made.[31] At that time two complete grisaille panels depicting the king and queen were on exhibit in the Musée de Tonnerre, encased in wooden frames that they had acquired while in the possession of Camille Dormois in the nineteenth century. This pair survives (see Figs. 42B, 49A), but two other lozenges representing the royal couple (Fig. 41), published in photos by Ernest Petit in 1898,[32] apparently do not. A 'collector's panel' now in storage at the Musée des Ursulines, Mâcon, contains fragmentary heads of a queen and two kings (Fig. 43).[33]

Following is a complete list of the Tonnerre glass that survives, plus the two lost heads (Fig. 41) known only from Petit's 1898 photos.

---

[30] The restorer was A. David, a glazier active at Auxerre from 1891-1939. A photo signed E. Lenoble shows a restored lancet containing six grisaille panels, those in the lancet head a queen and king within Group 4 borders; below them, a queen and king in Group 3 borders; and at the bottom, arms of Bourgogne and Anjou in Group 1 borders. Some of these panels were destroyed in 1940. I am grateful to Mme Anne-Bénédicte Clert, Conservateur délégué des Antiquités et Objets d'art de l'Yonne, for so generously sharing with me this photo and other information in her files.

[31] I examined the surviving panels in storage in 1994. I would like to thank the glazier M. Weinling and Terryl Kinder for their gracious assistance. On the Tonnerre fragments see *L'Art au temps des rois maudits* p. 387; Recensement III pp. 21, 203 (entry not entirely accurate); Annick Beau and André Matton, "Iconographie tonnerroise, Vitraux du vieil hôpital représentant les portraits de Marguerite de Bourgogne et de son époux Charles Ier d'Anjou," *Bulletin annuel de la Société d'archéologie et d'histoire du Tonnerrois* no. 26 (1973) pp. 51-55 (all illustrations are reversed but the queen on p. 53). Color illustrations: *Le Vitrail en Bourgogne: miroir du quotidien*, Images du patrimoine no. 23 (Dijon: 1986) p. 56; Line Skórka and Jean-Pierre Fontaine, *Tonnerrois*, (Rennes: 1992) p. 10; Quénée, front cover (caveat: this is a composite view combining the lozenge from Inv. no. 14 with a flopped photo of the grisaille Inv. no. 21).

[32] Petit, *Histoire* VI p. 480.

[33] Recensement III p. 101; in 1994 the panel was no longer on exhibit and was inaccessible for examination. Another 'collector's panel' from the hospital of Tonnerre is in storage at the Musée historique de Troyes et de la Champagne (Hôtel de Vauluisant), and was included in their catalog of 1864: Recensement IV p. 292. None of the four elements in it are related to the ensemble being discussed here. The silver-stained fleur de lis is certainly later; the woman's head includes two letter a's (not in gothic script).

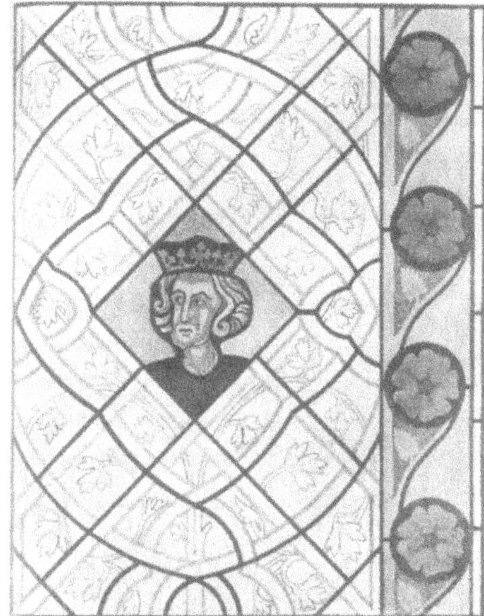

Fig. 38. Tonnerre. Drawing by Edmond Socard of grisaille panel. (After *Bulletin monumental* 1913).

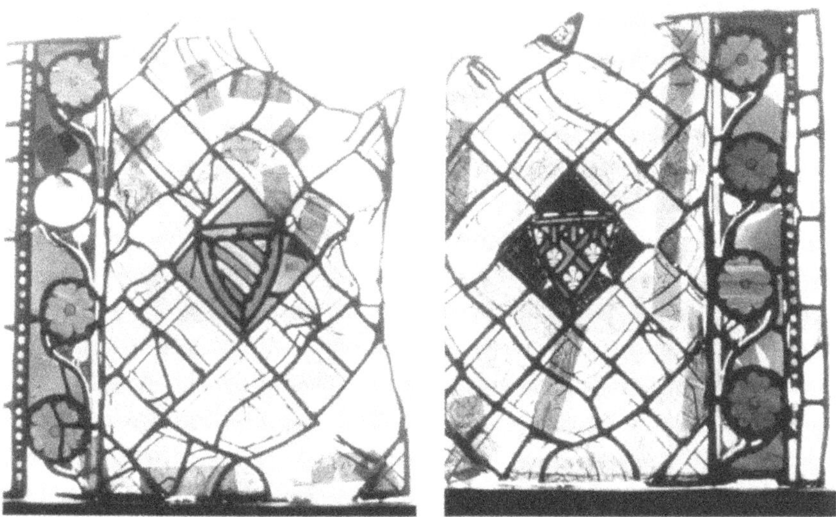

Fig. 39. Tonnerre. Grisaille panels with coats of arms of Burgundy and Anjou, and borders of marguerites. Ca. 1293-95. Inventory nos. 27 (left), 26/1 (right). (Photo: Lillich)

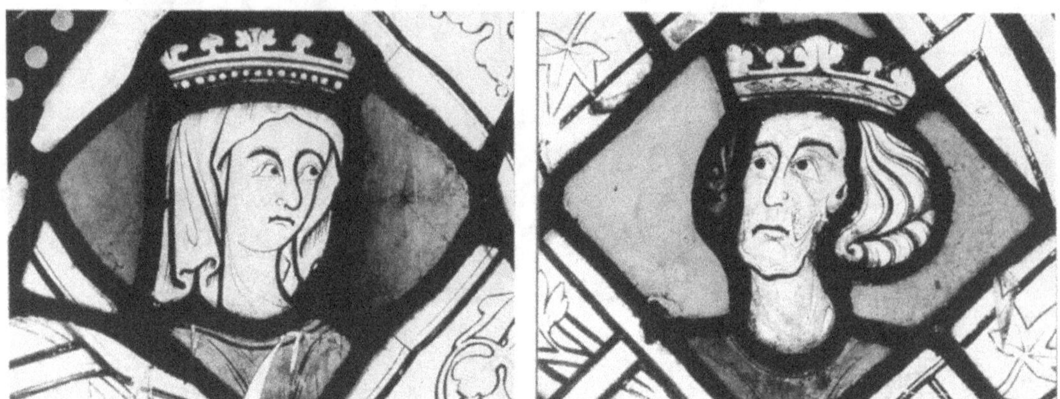

Fig. 40. Tonnerre. Heads of Marguerite de Bourgogne and Charles d'Anjou. Ca. 1293-95. Inventory nos. 14 (left), 18 (right). (Photo: Patrick Garrigue, Inventaire général 1986)

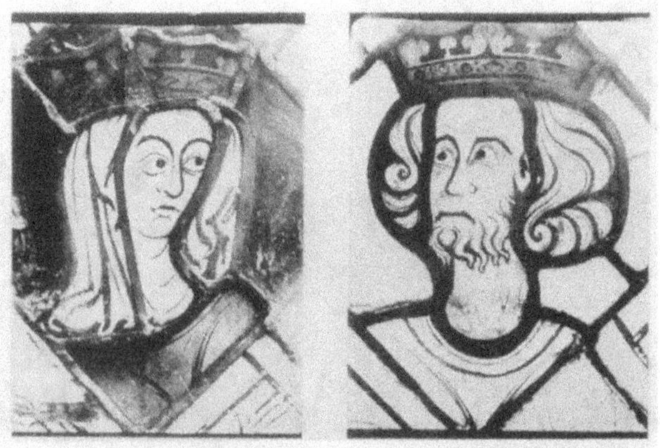

Fig. 41. Tonnerre. Heads (now lost) of Marguerite de Bourgogne and Charles d'Anjou. Ca. 1293-95. (After Petit, vol. VI, 1898)

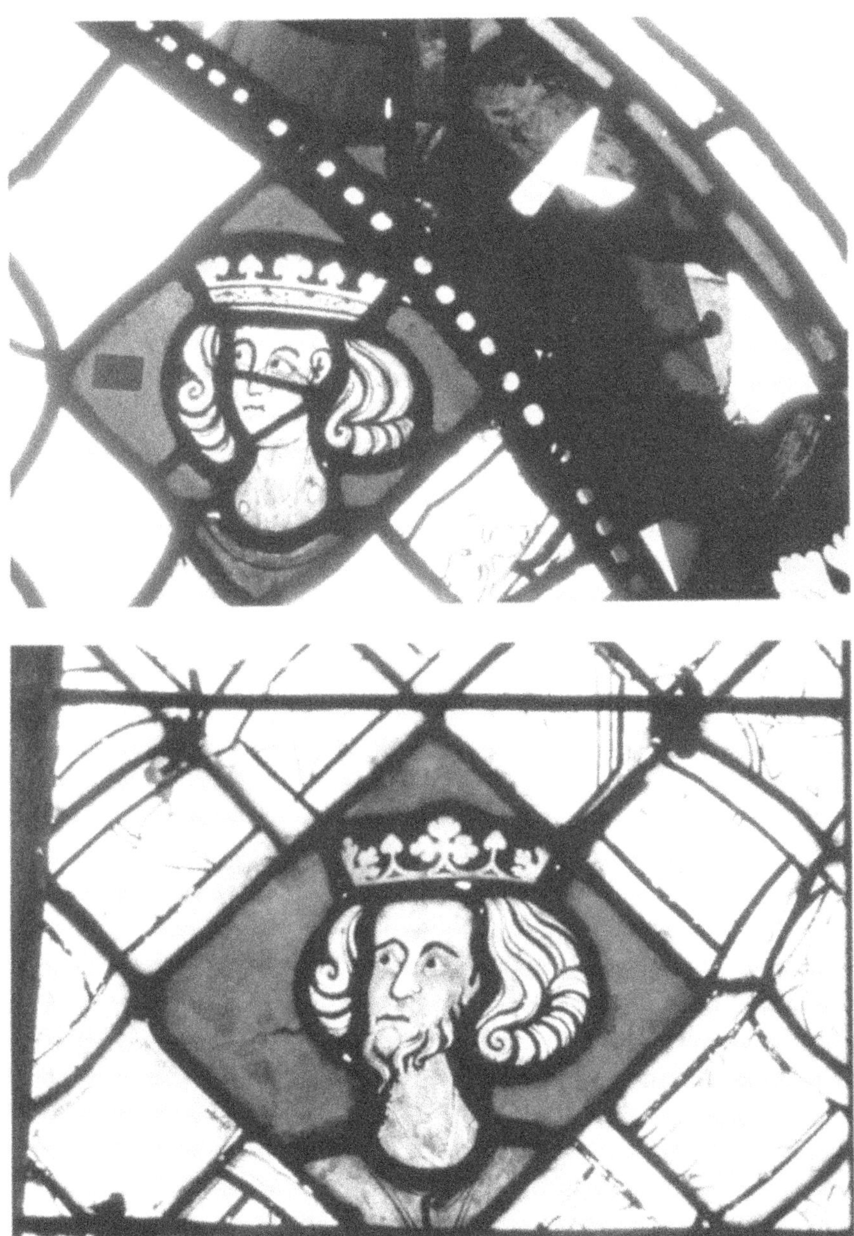

Fig. 42. Tonnerre. Heads, Charles d'Anjou. Inventory nos. 24 (above), 21 (below). Ca. 1293-95. (Photo: Lillich).

Elements are arranged below by design, with panels and debris of the same pattern grouped together. Numbers from the 1974 inventory are included.

COLORED GLASS FROM THE TRACERIES OF THE EASTERN CHAPELS

Square panels forming the centers of the quatrefoil lights

Four survive:
— "Green Man" (mask sprouting foliage)[34] on a blue ground, brown stems with yellow maple-like leaves. Inventory no. 2. (Fig. 44A)
— Red ground, interlocking pattern of filets formed of a white quatrelobe, yellow quatrelobe, and blue square. Inventory no. 3.
— Red ground, green stems forming a cross, with yellow maple-like leaves. Inventory no. 4. (Fig. 44B)
— Debris of a fourth square colored panel, not described further in the 1974 inventory, no. 13.

Colored lobes of the quatrefoils

Nine survive:
— two lobes: red ground, a white traceried "rose window." Inventory nos. 5, 6. (Fig. 45A)
— three lobes: red ground, a white traceried, six-pointed star. Inventory nos. 7, 9, 12 (12 = 9bis). (Fig. 45B)
— three lobes: red ground, branching yellow stem with green leaves and white grapes. Inventory nos. 8, 15, 16. (Fig. 46A)
— one lobe: blue ground, branching green stem with yellow leaves of naive design. Inventory no. 10. (Fig. 46B)

---

[34] Exhibited in *L'Art au temps des rois maudits* p. 387 no. 299. On the *masque feuillu* in thirteenth-century France see Kathleen Basford, *The Green Man* (Ipswich: 1978) pp. 15-17, pls. 24-32. She notes (p. 21) that the foliate head often is associated with tombs and memorials and may signify resurrection. A different interpretation is offered in Anthony Weir and James Jerman, *Images of Lust, Sexual Carvings on Medieval Churches* (London: 1986) pp. 105-8. The Tonnerre example is not humanoid but an animal mask and likely to be pure ornament.

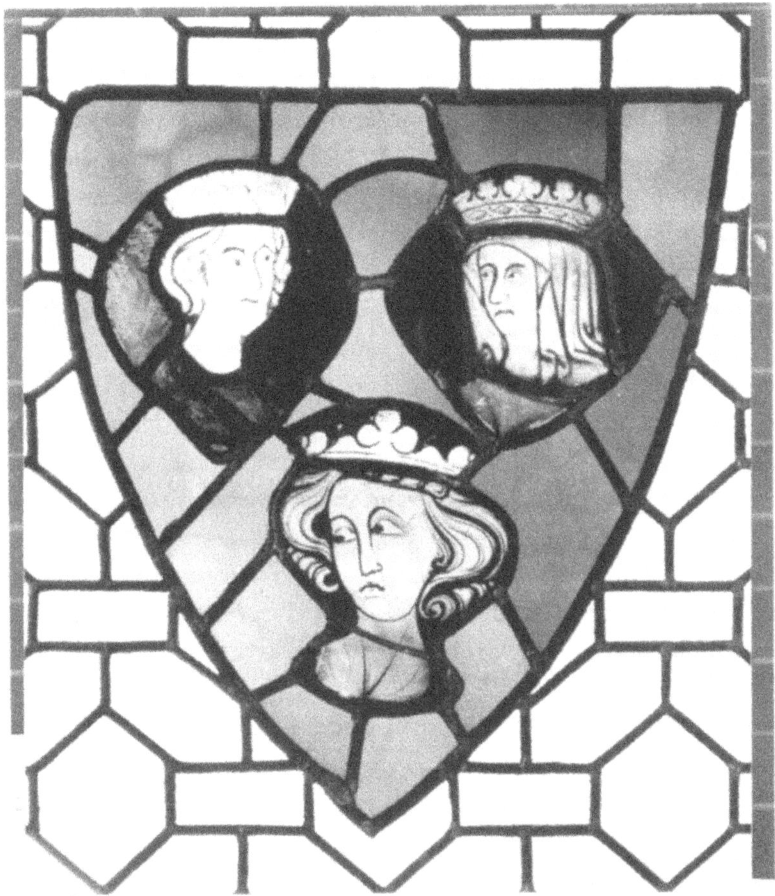

Fig. 43. Collector's panel composed of fragments of heads from Tonnerre, Hôtel-Dieu. Mâcon, Musée des Ursulines. (Photo: Patrick Garrigue, Inventaire général 1986)

GRISAILLE PANELS

Four border patterns survive, each accompanying a different type of foliage in the grisaille. The grisaille design of filets and foliage is otherwise uniform throughout. Uppermost panels, in the lancet heads, curve on one side, and the location of the border further allows for identification of panels as left, right, and bottom. A colored lozenge forms the central accent of each panel, though in some cases they are now missing. The lozenges repeat four designs: the queen's head, the king's head, and their coats of arms. Her arms are those used by her father, Eudes de Bourgogne, who died before becoming duke; thus they are Burgundy (*une bande d'or et d'azur à la bordure de gueules*) differenced by making the border *engrelée*. The arms of Charles d'Anjou, brother of the king of France, are *France* (*d'azur semé de fleurs de lis d'or*) differenced with a *lambel de gueules*.[35] Those lozenges that have become separated from their panels will be included at the end under Miscellaneous.

Group 1: eight panels survive. Borders of red marguerite flowers on a yellow stem, blue ground; foliage of notched leaves of five points.
— left panel: queen, yellow robe, red ground. Panel owned by Camille Dormois. Inventory no. 20.
— left panel: arms of Burgundy, blue ground. Inventory no. 27. (Fig. 39A)
— left bottom panel: arms of Burgundy. Inventory no. 17.
— right lancet head: king, red robe, blue ground. Inventory no. 18. (Fig. 40B)
— right panel: king, brown robe, blue ground. Panel owned by Camille Dormois. Inventory no. 21. (Figs. 42B, 49A)
— right panel: arms of Anjou, matte ground with stickwork diaper. Inventory no. 25.
— right panel: arms of Anjou, matte ground with stickwork diaper. Inventory no. 26. (Fig. 39B)
— right bottom panel: lozenge gone. Inventory no. 28.

[35] Arms of Eudes de Bourgogne: Anselme I p. 544. Arms of Charles d'Anjou: *Rolls of Arms* p. 167 (Walford's Roll).

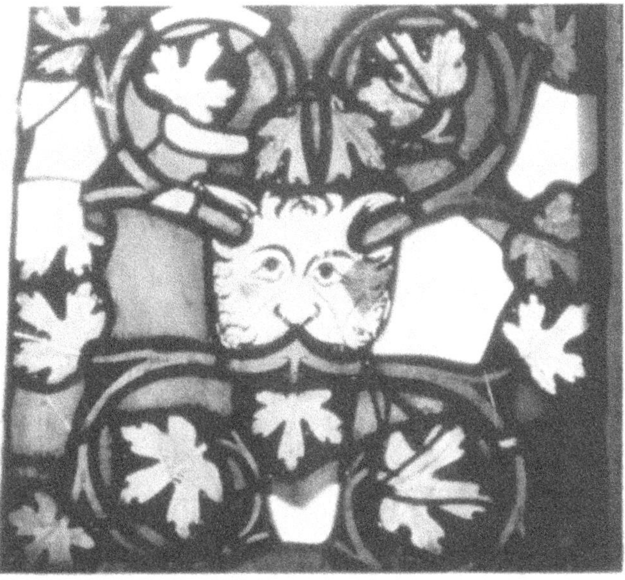

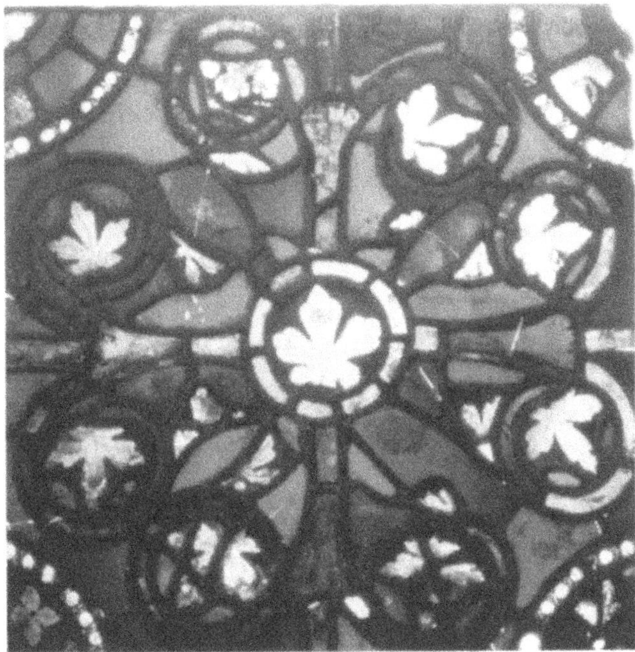

Fig. 44. Tonnerre. East chapels, square panels from tracery lights. Ca. 1293-95. Inventory nos. 2 (above), 4 (below). (Photo: Lillich).

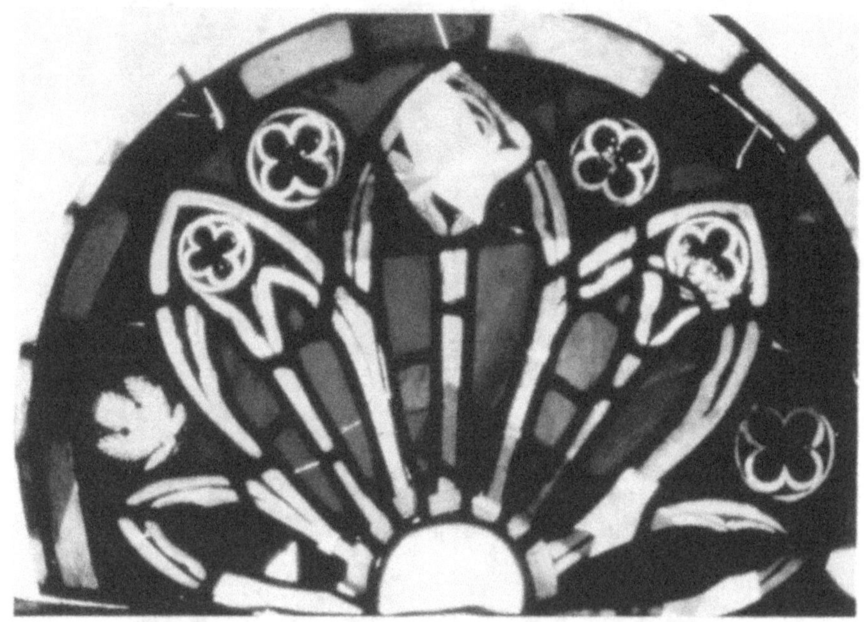

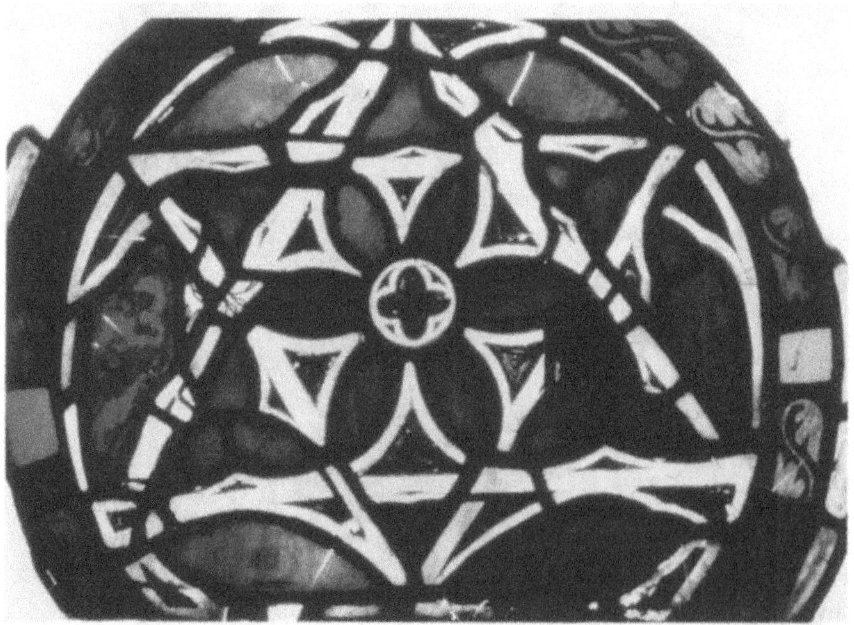

Fig. 45. Tonnerre. East chapels, lobes from tracery lights. Ca. 1293-95. Inventory nos. 5 (above), 9 (below). (Photo: Lillich).

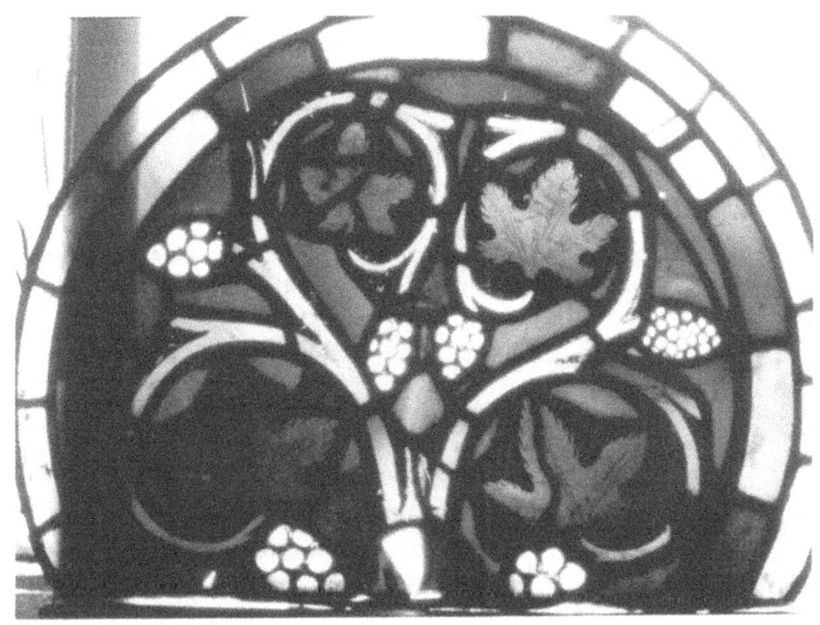

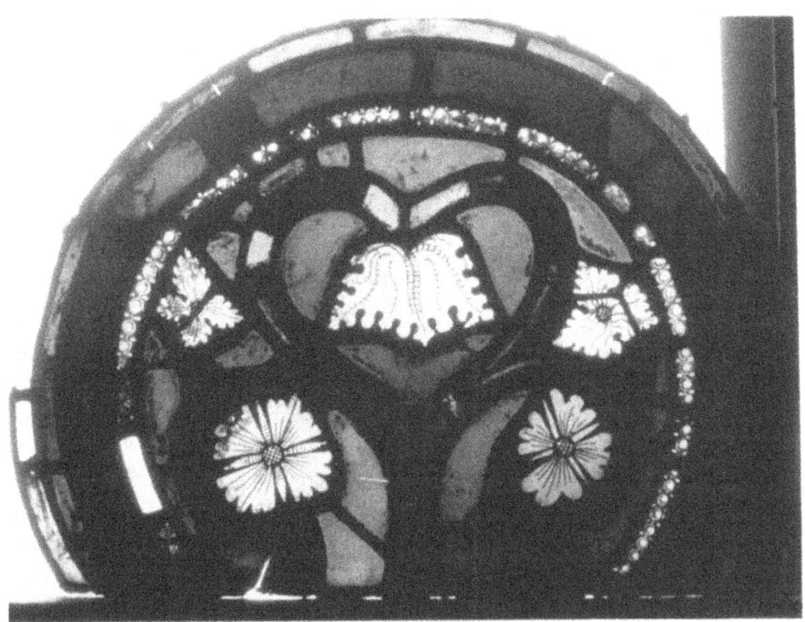

Fig. 46. Tonnerre. East chapels, lobes from tracery lights. Ca. 1293-95. Inventory nos. 8 (above), 10 (below). (Photo: Lillich).

Group 2: two panels survive. Charming, eccentric border of harpies (white, tan, rose-brown) with female heads, bird bodies and leaf-tails.[36] Blue ground. Foliage of five-pointed notched leaves with wavy outlines.
— left lancet head: lozenge gone. Inventory no. 23.
— right lancet head: lozenge gone. Inventory no. 22. (Fig. 47)

Group 3: two panels survive. Borders of undulating leaf-bundles of abstract white leaves, red ground; geranium-like fringed foliage in the grisaille.
— left panel: lozenge gone. Inventory no. 29. (Fig. 48)
— right panel: king, red robe, blue ground. Inventory no. 19.

Group 4: two panels survive. Border is a naive design probably by the same glazier who made the lobe with the blue ground. Thick yellow undulating filet with yellow and green leaves, red ground. The grisaille foliage is similarly unsophisticated: three-notched lobes, each with a little berry at the end.
— left lancet head: queen, green robe, red ground. Inventory no. 14. (Fig. 40A)
— right lancet head: king, brown robe, blue ground. Inventory no. 24. (Figs. 42A, 49B)

Miscellaneous elements — queen and king: lost. Photos published by Petit in 1898.[37] (Fig. 41)
— queen and two kings: in 'collector's panel', Musée des Ursulines, Mâcon. The queen and the king with stopgap crown appear to be set into the panel backwards, with paint side out.[38] (Fig. 43)

---

[36] Similar harpies appear with heraldry in the tile pavement of the queen's adjoining château (Figs. 20, 21). See also the painted *salle aux écus* of the château de Ravel, owned by Pierre Flote and dated 1300-1: Paul Deschamps and Marc Thibout, *La Peinture murale en France au début de l'époque gothique ... (1180-1380)* (Paris: 1963) pp. 211-12, 217, pl. CXXXVIII, CXXXIX. Monsters in contemporary grisaille glass: Lillich, *Rainbow* pp. 39, 120; Antoine de Schryver, Yvette vanden Bemden and Guido Bral, *Gothic Grotesques in Ghent. The Medieval Stained-Glass Fragments found in the Dominican Monastery* (Courtrai: 1991) pp. 35-62, 91. On the *sirène-oiseau*: Terence Hanbury White, ed. and trans., *The Bestiary* (New York: 1960) pp. 134-35 (twelfth century); Victor-Henry Debidour, *Le Bestiaire sculpté en France* (Mulhouse: 1961) p. 225, ills. 1, 89, 106, 326.

[37] See n. 32 above.

[38] See n. 33 above. The larger king may be overpainted or a modern copy?

— arms of Burgundy, in circle of green ground, set in panel of modern quarries. Inventory no. 11.

— queen, in circle of blue ground, set in panel of modern quarries. Inventory no. 1. (Frontispiece) This head faces in the opposite direction from the other heads of queens, and unlike them it is painted entirely on white glass with no color used for the crown, robe, etc. The exterior of the glass is iridescent. It may be an element from a different type of ensemble, perhaps from the chapel or the flanking château.

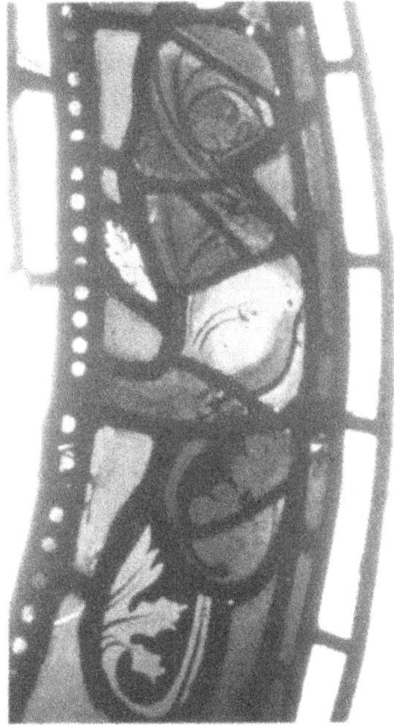

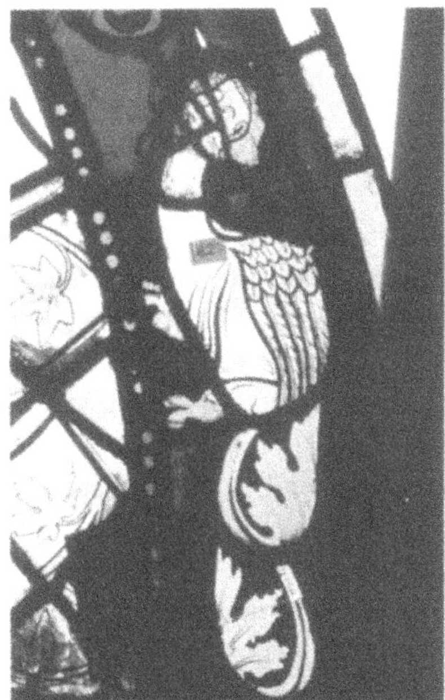

Fig. 47. Tonnerre. Grisaille panel with border of grotesques, details. Ca. 1293-95. Inventory no. 22. (Photo: Lillich).

Glass painters at Mussy and Tonnerre

If the ornament at Tonnerre (the related marguerite borders, and grisailles with the peculiar filet running along the lateral borders, both discussed earlier, Figs. 39, 49A) did not so closely match that at Mussy, it would not seem profitable to compare the handful of remaining heads from the hospital to the more monumental Mussy figures. The royal heads are a good deal smaller, occupying squarish lozenges around five and a half inches (14 centimeters) on a side. Glaziers, like all artists, alter and adapt their style to differing scales and it has been very difficult for art historians to attempt stylistic comparisons between small and large scale.[39] Moreover, there clearly are several craftsmen at work in each ensemble.

At Mussy, there are two distinct styles.[40] Most of the figural glass is the work of the remarkable and talented master responsible for the unforgettable, expressionistic axial Crucifixion and for the equally powerful kneeling figure of Bishop Gui de Genève (Figs. 13, 15-16). He uses a simple palette of primaries of strong, even brilliant, saturation— nothing subtle about it. His painting combines wash and a variety of thicknesses of trace line in beautifully detailed ornament and in modeling that defines the body structure. He occasionally achieves a fine spatial effect, as in the Crucifixion group (the cross in front of the framing border, the Virgin's wringing hands). His particular 'signature,' as pointed out by Pinto, is a fall of drapery defined at the hem by an inverted T-fold. The eyes are lengthened to a tear-drop finish and are often startlingly asymmetrical (Fig. 16). The eyebrow, detailed with rising vertical hairs, extends into a long straight nose with narrow base. The facial expressions achieve a riveting focus.

The other artist at Mussy seems to have been responsible for a single commission, that of the kneeling bourgeois couple now in Bay 101 (Fig. 14), and the Virgin (now in Bay 104) to whom they probably were praying originally.[41] This artist uses a very cool mannerist palette: no yellow at all, purple, an unusual rose for flesh tones, a muted deep red, and—most

[39] On the differences between large and small-scale work of a single glazier see Virginia Raguin, "The Visual Designer in the Middle Ages: The Case for Stained Glass," *Journal of Glass Studies* XXVIII (1986) pp. 30-39.

[40] Pinto (thesis pp. 92-96) also made this observation. A color plate of the axial Crucifixion appears in Recensement IV, pl. VIII opp. p. 141.

[41] The Virgin's head is an old restoration while the Child's, also replaced, has silver stain. The plated blue that this artist uses (see n. 42 below) appears in the lower drapery of the Virgin. Pinto pp. 33, 89, 91, 95-96.

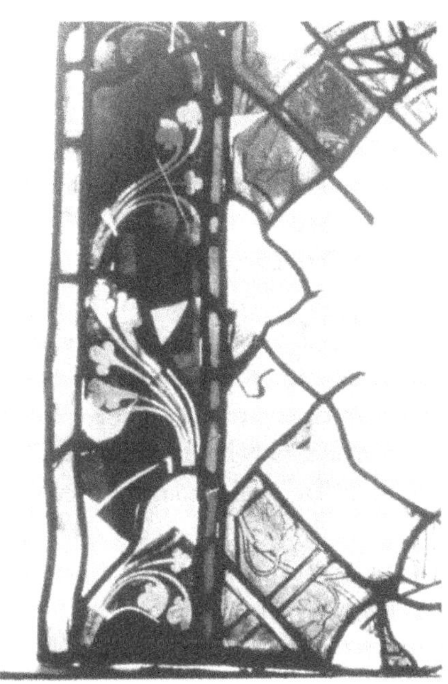

Fig. 48. Tonnerre. Grisaille panel with border of foliage, detail. Ca. 1293-95. Inventory no. 29. (Photo: Lillich).

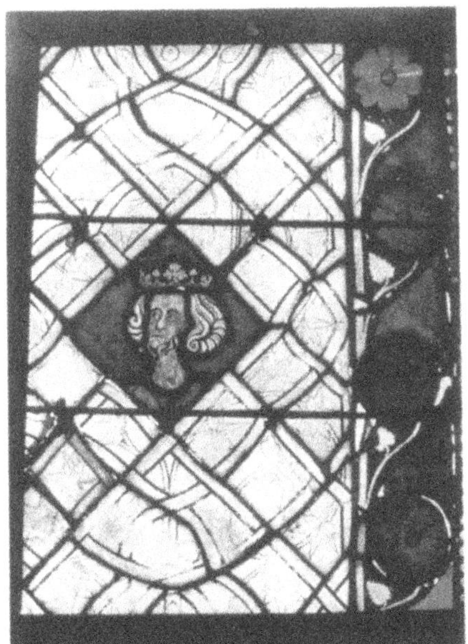

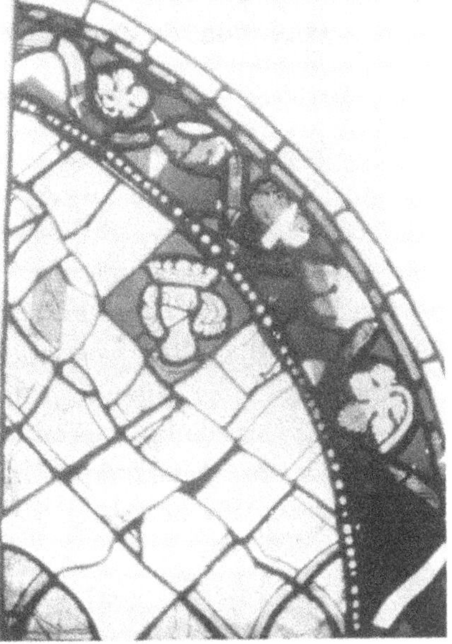

Fig. 49. Tonnerre. Grisaille panels with heads of Charles d'Anjou. Ca. 1293-95. Inventory nos. 21 (left), 24 (right). (Photo: Lillich)

extraordinary—a clear blue that is the earliest known example of a flashed blue glass (plated of blue and white).[42] The painting is not refined, indeed almost crude. The thick trace lines are fussy, and meaninglessly placed on the shapeless draperies. The lines outlining the eye do not close at the end, and the nose is broad at the base. In sum, the painting is as fussy and mannered as the cool color palette. He has nothing of his co-worker's fire, control, or careful finish.

At Tonnerre, it is hopeless to attempt a definitive judgment on the basis of a dozen often fragmentary heads from a program that originally had, perhaps, well over 300. The heraldically based colors are closer to the Mussy expressionist. The painting is generally related to that master as well. The diversity of crowns is truly remarkable, the king now bearded now clean-shaven, and indeed considerable effort has been expended to achieve a great variety of faces all made from the same pair of cartoons. The cartoons were undoubtedly provided by the first Mussy master, since many of his mannerisms appear: vertical hairs on the eyebrow, long straight nose with narrow base, asymmetrical eyes, T-fold hemline of the queen's veil. The finest heads (see Figs. 40, 41B, 42) could be by his hand: they share with Mussy the finish of detail, the flagrant and expressionistic asymmetry, and the remarkable focus. One of the heads of the queen, on the other hand, matches the characteristics of the second Mussy master closely (Fig. 41A). One is justified in concluding that the glaziers and architect of Mussy went to Tonnerre together to work on Marguerite de Bourgogne's great project of 1293-95.

The Familiar and the Other

One glass painter of Tonnerre worked only there: the folk artist who produced the naive patterns in the blue lobe and the grisailles of Group 4 (Figs. 46B, 49B). He is what art historians used to call a 'primitive,' an untutored artist who glories in pattern making, as often found in the art of children. In a medium as technically complex as stained glass, such folk expression is close to unknown.[43] Under the present circumstances there is no way to even guess how large was his part in the Tonnerre campaign,

[42] Jean-Jacques Gruber in Marcel Aubert et al, *Le Vitrail français* (Paris: 1958) p. 317 n. 50.

[43] A comparable anomaly is the naive folk artist at Sées cathedral, whom I have dubbed "The Primitive of Sées": Lillich, *Armor* pp. 212-13. He too employed cartoons in common use in the main atelier there.

but he was there and he worked with the main atelier, since his heads and grisailles employ cartoons identical with the others.

This *rara avis* can serve as a reminder of just how fundamentally different are the two monuments of Mussy and Tonnerre. Most of the norms of Gothic church building and glazing are observed at Mussy, which takes its place in the continuum of religious art of its period and region. Tonnerre is unique: not merely the solitary hospital of its period in France to survive, but one for which one can reasonably reconstruct the original program of its glazing decor. Tonnerre provides a precious glimpse through a small keyhole at the forgotten landscape of Gothic secular monumental arts. When one sees how basic 'portraiture' and heraldry are at Tonnerre, it should not be surprising that life-size donors resplendent in heraldic finery are at the same moment taking their places in Gothic church windows. The exquisite beauty and sophistication of the grisailles of Tonnerre, the delicacy of the traceried decoration in the lobes, the fun of the "Green Man" and of the female sirens stalking the Group 2 borders, testify to the vitality and verve of a secular art that we, seven centuries later, scarcely have the privilege to savor.

PART IV
THE ENSEMBLE AT MUSSY RECONSTRUCTED

Returning to Mussy, one may now attempt to reconstruct the original glazing program, from the perspectives of iconography, heraldry, and style, not to mention history—both archival and anecdotal. Except for the Cistercian-type grisailles, the style is homogeneous. While two artists are discernible, there is no chronological variance in their touch. Although the roundup restoration of 1740 jumbled survivors together (Figs. 4, 5), including various Renaissance elements from the church, the architecture of Mussy really does not offer so many apertures that one cannot make a reasoned guess at the original program. The transepts have no east or west fenestration (Fig. 51) and the fragments in the north transept facade contain silver stain,[1] thus indicating a later, fourteenth-century glazing campaign; certainly the original nave windows would have been no earlier.[2]

In addition to the five sides of the polygonal apse, there are only two lower windows on each side flanking the choir (Bays 5 to 8, the east and lateral openings of the choir aisles). There are only two clerestory bays on each side above (Bays 105-108), their triplet openings truncated at the bottom to accommodate the choir aisle roofs (Figs. 2, 4, 51-52). None of these lateral choir openings are really very easily seen, and the Baroque stalls and choir enclosure would have blocked them substantially more (Fig. 50). If a general comparison may be allowed to the glazing traditions

[1] North transept facade: Recensement IV p. 149 (Bay 109). Salet, "Mussy" p. 322, noted the unusual fact that the transepts have no windows except on the facades.

[2] The nave aisles lost their glass in the sixteenth century when chapels were added between the buttresses (see Fig. 50). The nave clerestory presents a puzzle: Arnaud (1837) p. 224 records doublet-and-rose windows there, which would be routine for Champagne—except for the fact that the Mussy choir has only triplet apertures. Morel-Payen (as in p. 58 n. 86) p. 200 observed that the present small, single lancets of the nave clerestory seem to have been set into large blinded bays. Part of the architectural stabilization of the late nineteenth century?

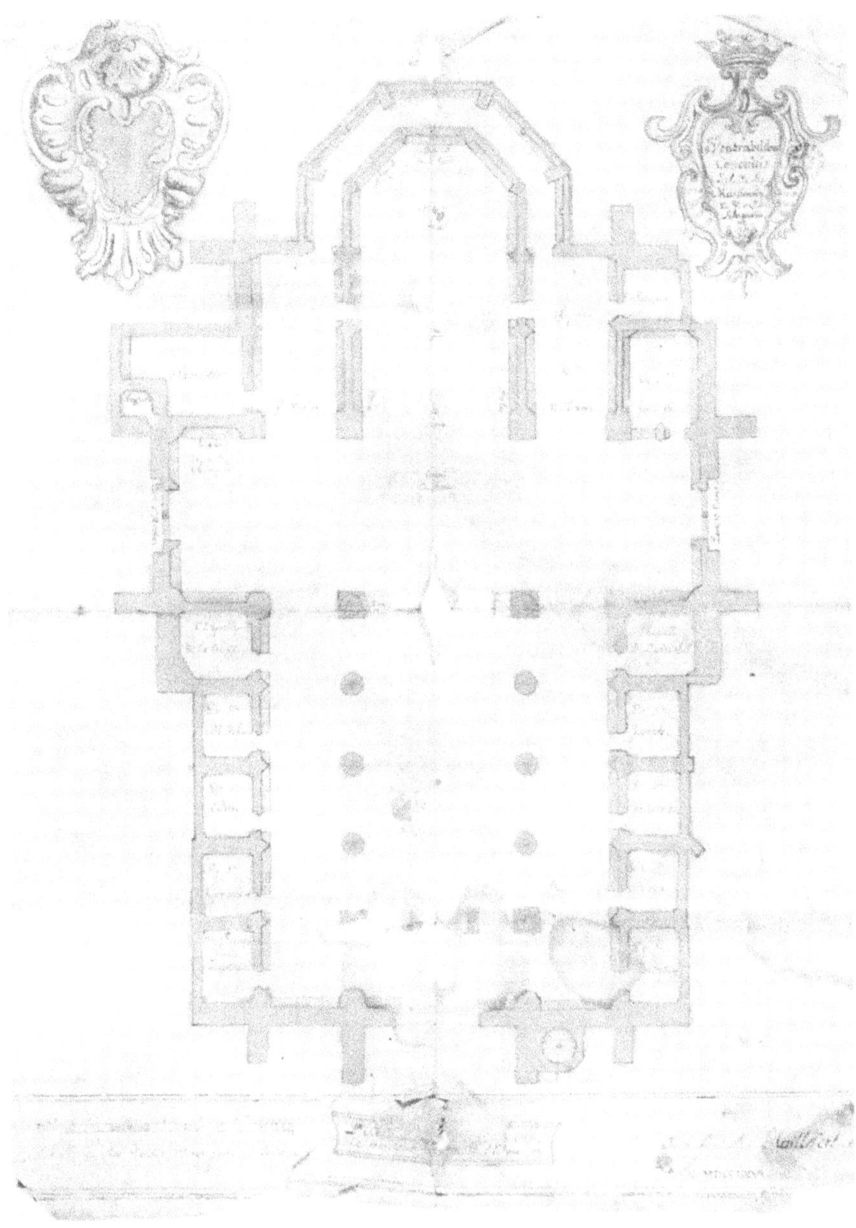

Fig. 50. Mussy. Plan of 1766 by Hier. Alex. Maillefert.Troyes, Bibliothèque municipale MS 3089, t. 3 fol. 1043 (papers of Charles Nioré). (Photo: Troyes, Bibliothèque municipale).

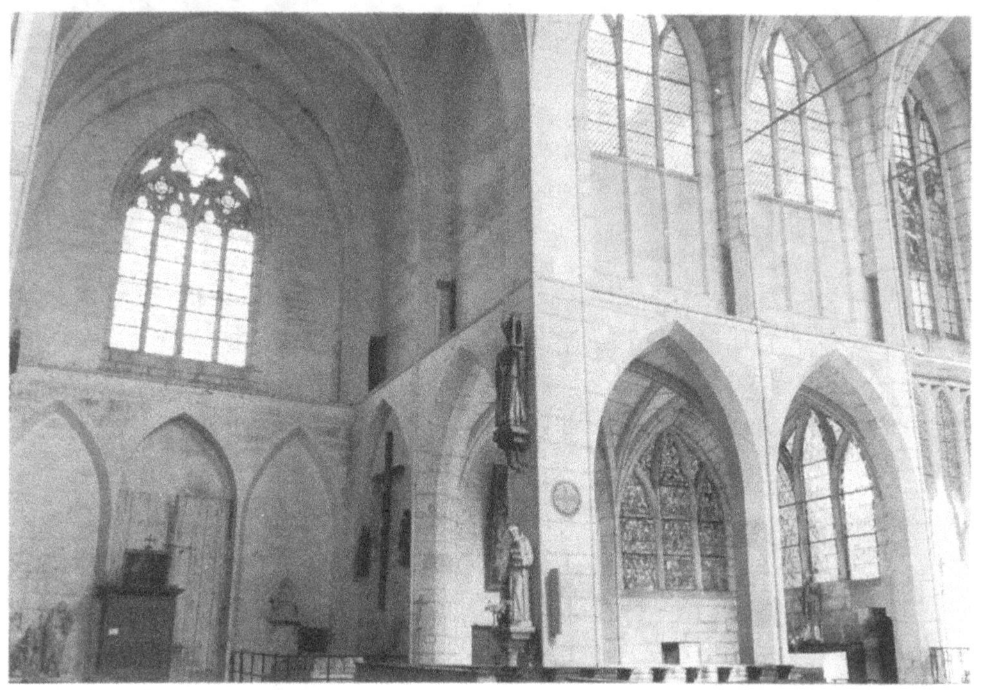

Fig. 51. Mussy. North transept; north choir showing clerestory Bays 107, 105 and part of 103, and north choir aisle Bays 7 and 5 (left to right). (Photo: S. Pearson, Conway Library).

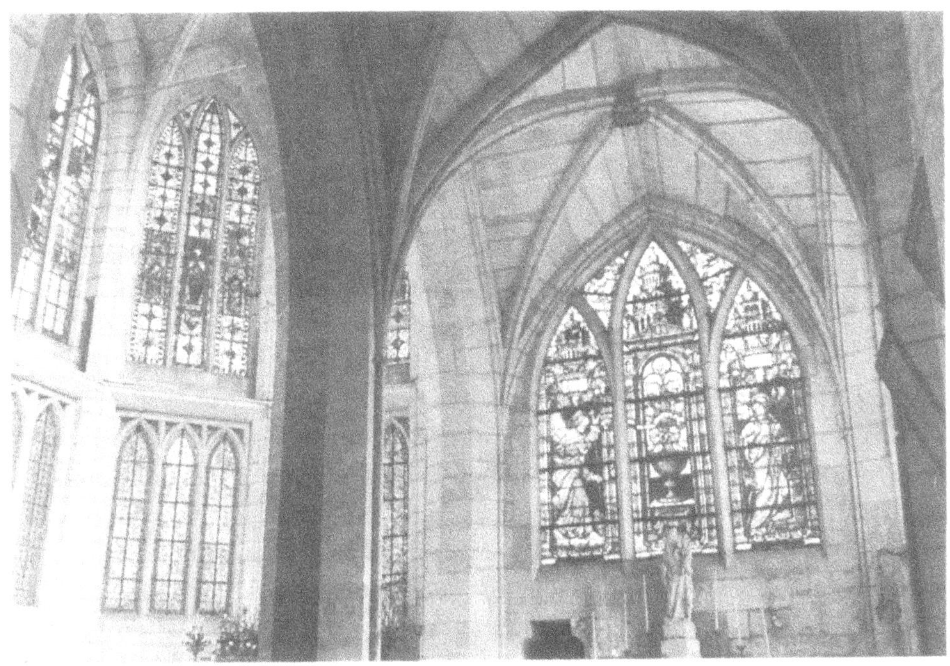

Fig. 52. Mussy. South choir aisle, Bay 6; visible to the left are north choir Bays 101 and 1, and part of clerestory Bay 103 (far left, Adam and Eve, sixteenth century). (Photo: S. Pearson, Conway Library).

of Lorraine, where churches likewise have no ambulatories,[3] one might expect grisailles in the side windows and color (perhaps in band windows as at present) in the showy apertures of the apse (Bays 100-104) and the east walls of the choir aisles (Bays 5, 6). The eastern bay of the south aisle (Bay 6) still contains a Renaissance window of the Annunciation (Fig. 52). It seems likely that the sixteenth-century Temptation of Adam and Eve (now in Bay 103, Figs. 51-52) was installed adjoining it in Bay 8, that is, in the southern, lateral fenestration of the aisle, and that it was 'rounded up' from there in 1740 to fill gaps in the highly visible Bay 102. That is where Didron found the Temptation (visible there in old photos, Fig. 4).

Only one element that may have occupied the north choir aisle opposite has so far been mentioned: the coat of arms of Jean de Rochefort (Fig. 25), then canon and treasurer of Langres (see p. 45). I have hypothesized that his shield was 'out of sight' in a closed chapel or behind partition walls hiding the choir aisles, when Fichot made his watercolors in 1840 and omitted it. To creep further out on this particular limb, Lambert in 1878 mentions among the debris he saw in the collage in the apse—not now surviving—that there were two Crucifixions (one in addition to axial Bay 100), "Les Saintes-Femmes" and other figures. These panels were probably medieval, since Lambert demonstrates that he could tell the difference; he states that the Renaissance Temptation of Adam and Eve looks more recent in date than the other glass.[4]

Thirteenth-century glazing ensembles never, as far as I know, display two large-scale images of the Crucifixion—and indeed it would be hard to imagine another in a bay flanking the riveting figure of the Crucifixus of Bay 100. Thus the second (lost) Crucifixion was undoubtedly small in scale, and perhaps the Holy Women Lambert mentions were represented at the tomb, in narrative sequence with it. The remains of a lost medallion cycle of the Passion? If such small-scale historiated glass filled a lower chapel window where small scenes would be appropriate (such as Bay 7, Fig. 51), it would have been herded into the apse in 1740 along with the Renaissance Adam and Eve directly opposite. And Didron would not

[3] Lillich, *Rainbow,* plans pp. 6, 31, 71.

[4] Lambert p. 371.

have included it, being a different scale, in his tidying up operation in the late nineteenth century. The Rochefort arms, pursuing this logic, would have remained behind and partially hidden, perhaps in an odd-shaped lancet-head panel of limited usefulness as a potential stopgap even by 1740 standards.[5]

I am assuming that the remaining figural glass was originally located in one of the bays of the polygonal apse, and that the short lateral clerestories (Bays 105-108, Fig. 51) contained grisailles, comparable to the arrangement in bays 101-102 of Saint-Gengoult, Toul.[6] There are five clerestories in the apse and five lower windows at Mussy, of which only the central three can really be seen well (Figs. 2-4); thus the remaining glass that was moved (to Bays 0-2 and 100-102) came from Bays 3, 4, 103, or 104. Next to be examined is the placement of glass in the collage in the central three bays prior to Didron's tidying up, using Pinto's diagram made from old photographs both interior and exterior (Figs. 4-5; Bay 103 is omitted in the diagram since no old photos remain for it.) The hodge-podge in the central three bays, to reiterate, was what Didron found—the glass that survived from the roundup of 1740, following subsequent damage in the Revolution.

A similar situation faced this author in studying Evron (Mayenne), where there was a documented roundup restoration ca. 1839 as well as an old photo illustrating it, followed by a tidying up restoration around 1900.[7] Those who herded together such collages of old glass did not radically move what was still there, but simply filled in the 'holes.' Faint evidence can thus be detected of the damaged (and 'bandaged') original format. In other words, one can employ a working assumption that a glass panel is in its original bay unless there is evidence to indicate otherwise, such as installation paint-side-out (a favorite mistake of the centuries when stained glass was not practiced in France).

---

[5] One possible location: the single small window in the Baptist chapel off the south transept (Fig. 50). The Baptist was of course Bishop Jean de Rochefort's name-saint. Another possibility: the double-curved lancet head at the center of Bay 7, north choir aisle (Fig. 51).

[6] Lillich, *Rainbow* pp. 30 (fig. 5), 36-37, pl. II.17.

[7] Lillich, *Armor* pp. 261-70.

Roll Call

Excluding the Rochefort arms discussed above (Fig. 25), the surviving elements at Mussy are:

— Crucifixion with Virgin and St John (three lancets, Fig. 13)
— Kneeling bourgeois couple (Fig. 14), stylistically grouped by Pinto with the Virgin now in Bay 104 (three lancets)
— Kneeling bishop Gui de Genève (Figs. 15-16)
— St Peter in Bay 102 (old glass only in head panel)
— Virgin and Child now in Bay 101 (old glass only in head panel)
— Frontal deacon (Fig. 18)
— Fragmentary inscription of Marguerite de Bourgogne (Fig. 28)
— Arms of Vienne (Fig. 22)
— Arms of de Mussy (Fig. 28)

To this list can be added the lost kneeling knight in heraldic surcoat, in the same de Mussy arms.

It seems clear from Pinto's diagram (Fig. 5) that the choir clerestory originally had band windows, as now, and that the gaps existing by 1740 were filled at that time largely above and below the figural band—at least in Bays 100 and 102. Bay 101 is more complicated, since the bourgeois donors were moved there (and installed backwards), and the Virgin they had been praying to was moved above the Crucifixus in Bay 100. The reconstruction would be, so far, as follows:

— Bay 100: Crucifixion with Virgin and St John, in original location (in situ)
— Bay 102: Bishop Gui praying to St Peter, patron saint of Mussy (in situ)
— Bay 104: Bourgeois couple praying to the Virgin

I would place the couple in Bay 104 because, as I have explained, I believe that they were herded into the trio of 'visible bays' from one of the less visible lateral bays (Bay 103 or 104)—and because something else must have been in Bay 103.

Bay 103 undoubtedly contained the lost kneeling figure of the knight in heraldic surcoat that so stimulated the imagination of Père Vignier ca. 1650. That bay was the location of the 'founder's tomb' according to

Arnaud (1837).[8] In his day, following the Revolution, it had been moved to the north transept but he states with authority that it had been located to the left of the altar, standing upright against the wall under the first window of the sanctuary (Bay 3) and that the base of the window had been blinded so the tomb would not extend over it. Originally, he submits, the tomb had been horizontal, and the canons raised it against the wall to get it out of the traffic pattern around the altar. That probably occurred during the extensive work ca. 1740.

There is abundant evidence that Gothic tombs were often located in proximity to stained glass images with the name and/or arms of the individual memorialized or of his family. Saint-Nicaise de Reims could be cited, in Champagne and exactly contemporary with Mussy.[9] The lost kneeling knight of Mussy was, I believe, in clerestory Bay 103, taking his place among all the kneeling donors up there (more extensive than at present, as I believe), while his matching shield (now in Bay 101, Fig. 28) was below him in the lower window, Bay 3, just above the tomb in its original horizontal placement. Around 1740 the shield was herded into the central apse, but what became of the lost kneeling knight? He was undoubtedly herded too, possibly into the then-empty lancet of Bishop Gui's window (Bay 102), and as a representative of the Ancien Régime, smashed in the Revolution. So one can add to the reconstruction-list above:

— Bay 103: kneeling knight in heraldic surcoat (lost)

The clerestory group, according to this hypothesis, would have been filled with large-scale donors praying to appropriate saints, though in the case of Bay 103 no hint remains of who the saint may have been.

The final remaining clerestory (Bay 101) is the most damaged and confused of the apsidal group. If, as I believe, the Mussy glass was donated in large part by Marguerite de Bourgogne, in some sort of conciliatory endeavor with Bishop Gui following the 1288 vandalism of Pothières, it is possible that her kneeling image occupied Bay 101, opposite the bishop

[8] Arnaud pp. 224-25.

[9] Lillich, "Heraldry and Patronage in the Lost Windows of Saint-Nicaise de Reims," *L'Art et les révolutions* VIII, 27e Congrès international d'histoire de l'art, 1989 (Strasbourg: 1992) pp. 81-82, 86, 89.

still in Bay 102 and at the right hand of the Crucified Christ still in the axial window. If Tonnerre is taken as a guide, she certainly never demonstrated any hesitancy about having her image on display in stained glass! And no doubt Charles d'Anjou would be kneeling with her, both of them resplendent in heraldry as at Tonnerre.

I am led to this hypothesis by several avenues. These figures would have been destroyed, not in the Revolution but long before—since had royal images been present in the seventeenth century, Père Vignier's imagination would not have been allowed such free flight. The Virgin that Queen Marguerite and Charles d'Anjou, I believe, were praying to still exists in their bay (101), and severely damaged, with a small amount of old glass still remaining only in the head panel. Anti-royalist vandalism at Mussy had had many opportunities. In the last stages of the Hundred Years' War, Mussy, loyal to the French king, was taken by the Burgundians in May 1431, retaken by Charles VII and held by his cruel captain Tristan l'Ermite, and in June 1433 besieged and taken by the Burgundian duke Philippe le Bon in person. In December 1440 Mussy was pillaged by the *écorcheur* Alexandre de Bourbon. In 1474, in the conflict between King Louis XI and the duke Charles the Bold, troups of the latter occupied Mussy for many months. During the Ligue, Mussy was held by the Ligueurs in the 1590s, and one of the canons was put to death for saying "Vive le Roy."[10]

My second avenue of approach to the original appearance of Bay 101 is provided by what might be called the 'new court style' in stained glass donations following the advent of Marie de Brabant as Philippe le Hardi's second queen in 1274. I have discussed elsewhere her glass commission for Saint-Nicaise de Reims in 1284-85 and its enormous impact on the fashion of aristocratic glazing donations to follow.[11] While no visual evidence

---

[10] Roserot, *Dictionnaire* II pp. 1010, 1016-17. The events of 1431-33: Roserot, ed., *Le Plus ancien registre des délibérations du conseil de ville de Troyes (1429-1433)* (Troyes: 1886) pp. 29-32 (= Collection de documents inédits III pp. 191-94). The siege by the duke of Burgundy in 1433 is recounted in *The Chronicles of Enguerrand de Monstrelet*, trans. Thomas Johnes I (London: 1840) pp. 617-18. On Alexandre de Bourbon 1440: Alexandre Tuetey, *Les Ecorcheurs sous Charles VII* I (Montbéliard: 1874) pp. 75-76. On the Ligue 1590-94, see *Mémoires de Jacques Carorguy, greffier de Bar-sur-Seine 1582-1595*, ed. Edmond Bruwaert (Paris: 1880) pp. 84-85, also 39, 107-8, 194.

[11] See n. 9 above.

remains of Queen Marie's window at Reims, its brabantine splendor can be imagined from a drawing of a lost window in her family's burial chapel in Louvain which she commissioned in 1274/76 (Figs. 53-54). On this basis one may proceed with the hypothesis at Mussy. First to factor the elements of the ensemble at the brabantine chapel: grisaille of bulged quarries; heraldic borders; kneeling figures with inscription bands, under canopies; coats of arms below; the Crucifixion with Mary and John; two saints meaningful to the people involved. These elements are strikingly close to the Mussy ensemble that I propose as the queen of Sicily's gift, that is, Bays 100 and 101 (and probably the bays below them): Crucifixion with Mary and John; kneeling donors, now lost; heraldry. The fragmentary inscription in Bay 101 is thus in its original window. The missing lower panels of Bay 1 below it (see Fig. 5 diagram) may even have contained a series of shields of Anjou and Bourgogne, as was to be at Tonnerre.

May one take the next leap of faith and try to place the frontal deacon (now in Bay 102) in this landscape? Clearly he is a central, axial figure! A comparably frontal deacon (the patron St Stephen) appears along with the Crucifixion in the axial bay of the cathedral of Châlons-en-Champagne. The most central location remaining in Mussy is immediately below the Crucifixus—that is, in Bay 0. Bay 0 was blinded, probably for stability in 1740, and its glass would then have been moved, in the 'roundup' then in progress, somewhere within the three central bays. I propose that the deacon panels were simply bumped one bay over, into Bay 2, where they appear in nineteenth-century photos (see Figs. 4-5). He would have formed a stunning axial focus to the church, with grisaille matching that of the clerestory bay above, and no doubt more heraldry of Marguerite and Charles below (since the lower panels were destroyed by the nineteenth century, as indicated in the diagram of Bay 2 in Fig. 5).

The Mysterious Deacon

The question still remains of who the deacon is (Fig. 18). He has never been identified satisfactorily. He has no halo—though since the head has been carefully copied in modern times, one cannot be absolutely certain he never had one. He appears in deacon's dalmatic, but nothing

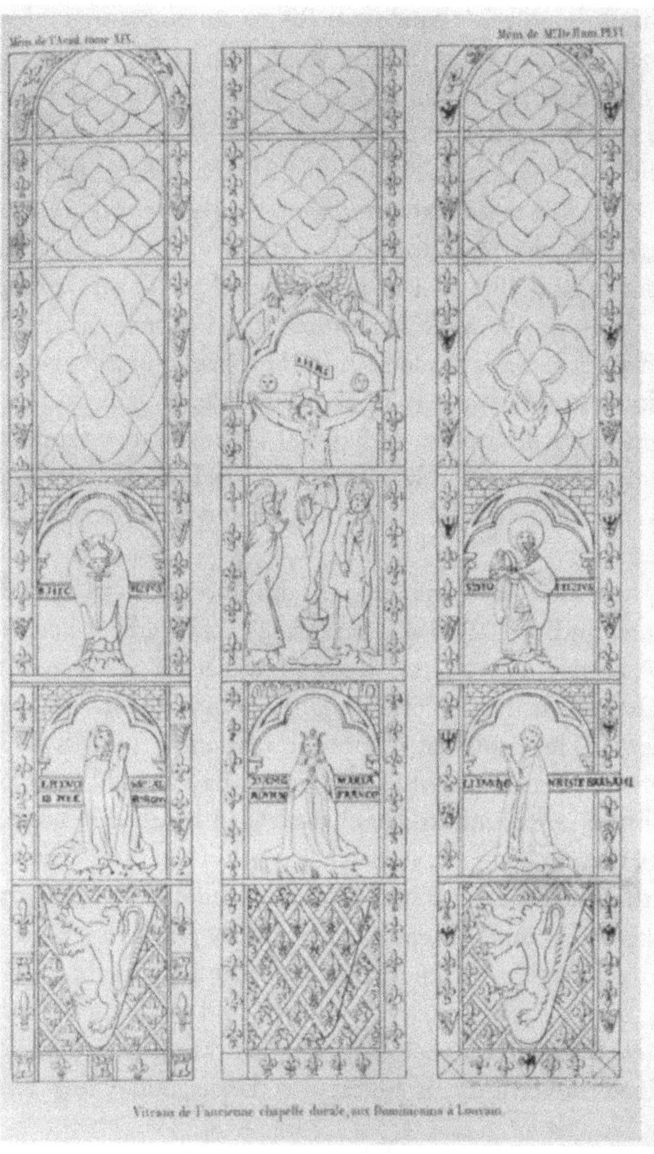

Fig. 53. Window of Queen Marie de Brabant. Ca. 1274/76 (destroyed 1637). Louvain, Dominican church, ducal chapel. (After de Ram, 1845)

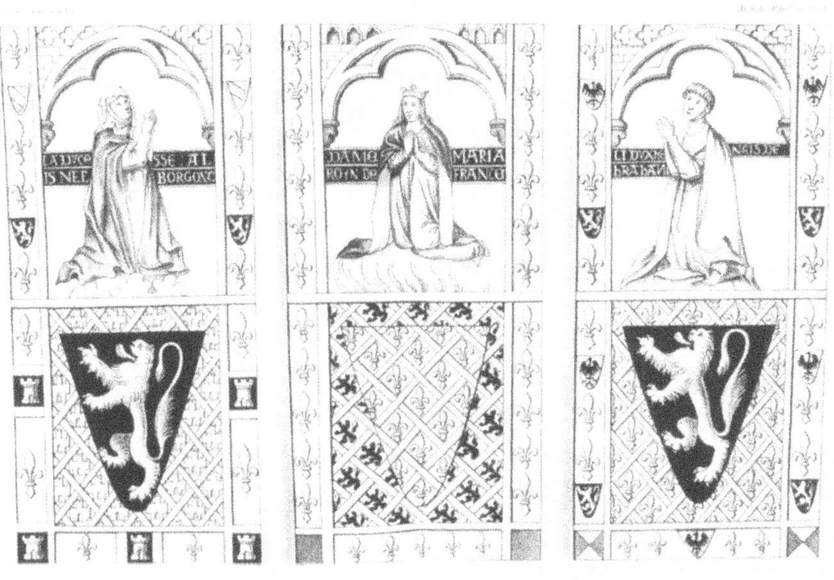

Fig. 54. Window of Queen Marie de Brabant, detail. Ca. 1274/5. Louvain, Dominican church. (After de Ram, 1845)

at Mussy suggests that he might represent one of Ecclesia's great trio of deacon martyrs (Stephen, Vincent, Lawrence). I propose that he, most probably, is St Vallier (Valerius, Valère), archdeacon to St Didier, the venerable fourth-century bishop martyr of Langres.

There was a church dedicated to St Vallier in Tonnerre on the mount near the château of the counts, Marguerite de Bourgogne's principal base of operations in the decade 1285-95. At Langres cathedral the image of St Vallier was carried before the *grand archidiacre* in solemn processions.[12] Although some discrepancy exists among the standard references, it is

[12] On St Vallier see *Bibliotheca sanctorum* XII (Rome: 1969) col. 920. The church of Saint-Vallier in Tonnerre was destroyed before 1414, in the wars between France and the English and Burgundians, according to Robert Luyt, *La Découverte d'un saint caché en la ville de Tonnerre, ou l'histoire de saint Micomer* (Sens: 1657) p. 141. On the Langres processions: Denis Gaultherot, *L'Anastase de Lengres* (Langres: 1649) p. 205; Blaise Caillet, *Vie des saints du diocèse de Langres* (Langres: 1873) p. 443.

demonstrable that the relics of St Vallier were at the Benedictine abbey of Saint-Pierre de Molosme (*Melundense*), some six kilometers east of Tonnerre, where they had been placed for safekeeping at some time before A.D. 992.[13] Indeed it is even possible that Langres was hatching a plot to get Vallier's relics back. In 1307 the bishop had them authenticated during a ceremony in which the body and head were separated, the body translated to a new *châsse* and the head to a bust reliquary.[14]

There is a further and more sensitive aspect to St Vallier's selection and appearance, beyond the lack of halo. He is garbed in the typical vestment of a canon. One has only to peruse the Gaignières drawings of medieval canons' tombs to find numerous examples identical even to the book that he 'presents' with both hands—instead of the martyr's palm as might be expected.[15] The central placement of this totally frontal figure, in the central bay of the apse of Mussy behind the high altar, would have been right in the midst of the canons, who would have passed him many times during the course of a mass or office. The choice of such a saint from their diocese and his depiction as a canon like them seems

---

[13] On Molosme: Montrond (as in p. 73 n. 12) col. 538. The controversy has been over whether the abbey was Molosme or Molesme (*Molismus*), a Benedictine house in the same region founded in 1075 and dedicated to Notre-Dame. See the discussion in *Acta Sanctorum*, Octobris IX (Brussels: 1858) pp. 529-30, and the thorough investigation by Gabriel Dumay, "Des origines de l'église de Talmay, du temps et du lieu de la mort de saint Vallier, du sanctuaire ou son corps fut conservé jusqu'à la Révolution," *Bulletin d'histoire et d'archéologie religieuses du diocèse de Dijon* XII (1894) pp. 81-125. He concludes that it was Molosme (pp. 119, 121-24), citing among other documents one of 18 October 1307 (Arch. Côte-d'Or) specifying that the relics were in the church of Saint-Pierre in the monastery of Molosme (Molesme was dedicated to Notre-Dame).

My identification of the saint as Vallier could be maintained even were the location of his relics indeed Molesme, since that abbey was even closer to Mussy (about 12 km. southwest) and well known to Marguerite de Bourgogne: see her documents published in Petit, *Histoire* VI no. 4826 (Nov. 1287), no. 5117 (Feb. 1293). Vallier appears in the Molesme calendar of ca. 1250 with a 12-lesson feast, although he is missing from the calendar of ca. 1175: see Chrysogonus Waddell, *The Summer-Season Molesme Breviary* I (Trappist, Ky: 1985)p. 214; on the dates of the calendars, pp. xxxiv-xxv (MOL, EVR, JUL 1). Many thanks to Fr Chrysogonus for generous xeroxes and discussion.

[14] See previous note (Dumay p. 119); Mathieu p. 129.

[15] Adhémar (1974) nos. 229, 427, 449, 483, 523, 554, 585. On the martyr's palm as Vallier's attribute: Louis Réau, *Iconographie de l'art chrétien* III, *Iconographie des saints* (Paris: 1955), v. 3 p. 1307 (Vallier); *Lexikon der christlichen Ikonographie* VIII: *Ikonographie der Heiligen*, ed. Wolfgang Braunfels VIII (Rome: 1974) col. 533 (Valerius).

particularly thoughtful, something one might expect from the queen of Sicily.

Two Widowed Queens

But would Marguerite go along with the flashy heraldic display of the brabantine style of glazing? I think one can safely make that assumption, not only on the evidence of the 300 or more images of herself and her husband (accompanied by over 300 coats of arms) originally at Tonnerre, but also on the evidence of her close relationship to Marie de Brabant, queen of France. That gay intriguer, as Powicke has called her, was Marguerite's cousin, Marie's mother and Marguerite's father being siblings. Another sibling Robert, the reigning duke of Burgundy, had profited enormously from Marie's queenship, being named *grand chambrier* of France around 1277, and was among the most faithful and attentive of Marie's inner entourage. He and she had been present with Bishop Gui de Genève at the death of her husband, Philippe le Hardi, in Spain. Queen Marie also was intimate with the family of Jean de Rochefort, and in December 1289 successfully extracted a favor from the pope on behalf of Jean's nephew Gaucher de Rochefort. "Sage et belle, savante et spirituelle, dont les contemporains célèbrent les mérites," Queen Marie de Brabant was also a trusted friend of the queen of Sicily, who named her an executor of her will and in a codicil left her a sapphire.[16] The queen of Sicily herself was buried wearing a silver-shot silken robe, silver crown and silver medallion of the Virgin around her neck, and a gold and emerald ring.[17] The two queens may not have been so altogether different after all.

Both were widowed in the same year, 1285, and both retired to the country. Marie lived at her château behind the *collégiale* of Mantes, where around 1300 she built the so-called *chapelle de Navarre*, which contains

---

[16] Petit, *Histoire* VI pp. 29, 73, 144, nos. 5800, 5874; Le Maistre (1867) p. 87. Gaucher de Rochefort was under twenty in 1289, probably a younger son of Jean's brother Gaucher; he does not appear in the genealogical study by Roger, "Les Morhier champenois" pp. 101-3.

[17] Le Maistre (1867) p. 89. Some of her jewels are on exhibit at the Hôtel-Dieu: Quénée p. 78.

four marble statues of standing aristocratic women,[18] strikingly similar in type to the polychromed wooden statues surviving from Tonnerre (see Appendix II pp. 120-23 below). It is most likely that Marguerite de Bourgogne at Mussy followed the fashionable trend in glazing just introduced by her friend at Saint-Nicaise, as did Philippe le Bel, his queen Jeanne, Gaucher de Châtillon, the countess Jeanne de Toucy, and the gilded aristocracy of the succeeding generation. One only has to think of Evreux cathedral to recognize that life-size heraldically resplendent images and elaborate name inscriptions had come to stay.

Mussy, however, is not precocious but an expected stage in the development of French glazing programs in the 1280s. The new brabantine fashion introduced by Queen Marie de Brabant at Saint-Nicaise in Reims was really just a case of emphasis, since all elements (grisaille, large-scale donors under canopies, inscriptions, heraldry) were already present in French glass. One could cite the cathedral of Sées (Orne), solidly dated to 1270-85—years straddling the period when Queen Marie's 'new court style' was introduced—where eleven life-size donors, a few with inscriptions or heraldry, are depicted praying to a variety of saints, including the Virgin repeated three times.[19]

The Patron of Mussy: Not a Corrupt Man but a Virtuous Woman

To return to the hypothetical reconstruction of the original glazing program, based on the diagram of the nineteenth-century collage (Fig. 5) and the arguments above, I submit that the images were probably arranged as follows:

---

[18] For my argument see Lillich, "European Stained Glass around 1300: The Introduction of Silver Stain," *Europäische Kunst um 1300, Akten des XXV. Internationalen Kongresses für Kunstgeschichte* VI/6 (Vienna: 1986) pp. 47-52; the statues of the chapelle de Navarre, p. 50 and n. 56. For the more traditional hypothesis, with bibliography, see most recently *L'Art au temps des rois maudits* (as in p. 58 n. 87) pp. 132-33. The lancets of the chapelle were blinded in the nineteenth century and have since been filled with modern glass; fragments of old grisaille, heraldic borders and canopies remain. See *Les Vitraux de Paris, de la région parisienne, de la Picardie et du Nord-Pas-de-Calais*, Corpus Vitrearum France, Recensement I (Paris: 1978) p. 131, bays 24 and 26.

[19] Lillich, *Armor*, ch. VI pp. 177-78, 186-89, 193-96 passim.

- Bay 100: Crucifixion with Virgin and St John (Fig. 13, in situ), donated by the queen of Sicily
- Bay 0: St Vallier (Fig. 18), probably with matching grisaille to Bay 100 and lost lower row of coats of arms. Donated by the queen of Sicily
- Bay 101: Lost images of the queen of Sicily and her husband praying to the Virgin (parts of Virgin's head panel, as well as fragmentary inscription, survive in situ)
- Bay 1: Cistercian-type grisaille (Fig. 10, in situ) with marguerite borders like those at Tonnerre; lost heraldry in lower row. Gift of queen of Sicily
- Bay 102: Bishop Gui de Genève (Figs. 15-16) praying to St Peter (still in this bay). The image originally in the left lancet was probably lost by 1650; perhaps it depicted the bishop's grandniece Jeanne de Vienne in heraldic robe
- Bay 2: Cistercian-type grisaille; probably with shield of Jeanne de Vienne (Fig. 22, now in Bay 100, moved there in 1740 when the deacon saint was installed in Bay 2?)
- Bay 103: lost kneeling knight in heraldic surcoat of de Mussy (moved in 1740, lost in 1793?). Memorial to Gui de Mussy, killed in the Sicilian Vespers? Remainder of bay unknown
- Bay 3: Cistercian-type grisaille; arms of de Mussy (Fig. 28, now in Bay 101)
- Bay 104: bourgeois couple (Fig. 14, the mason Perrenet Barottier and his wife Jacquette?) praying to the Virgin
- Bay 4: Cistercian-type grisaille; perhaps their 'heraldry,' the lost coat of arms in Fichot's 1840 watercolor (Fig. 6 no. 3), was here? (see pp. 76-77)
- Bays 105 to 108: grisailles

While Marguerite de Bourgogne was not the only contributor to the bishop's building and glazing project in the late 1280s, she does appear as the dominant presence and one may assume that she had a say in the outcome—an up-to-date arrangement of images and motifs in the fashionable brabantine court style.

It is thus unfortunate in the extreme that current scholarly opinion has stated with such finality that the church was built and glazed by Guillaume de Mussy, the king's bailiff, "unscrupulous in his private affairs and ... harsh in enforcing royal right," in disgrace for his misdeeds from late

1292 until August 1298 but not necessarily present in Mussy.[20] By that time in any event the choir of the church was complete. We owe the beauties of Mussy not to a bad man but to a good woman, Marguerite de Bourgogne, whose epithet[21] eulogizes her as *humilitatis speculum, caritatis refugium, puritatis vestigium*: Mirror of humility—refuge of charity—abode of purity.

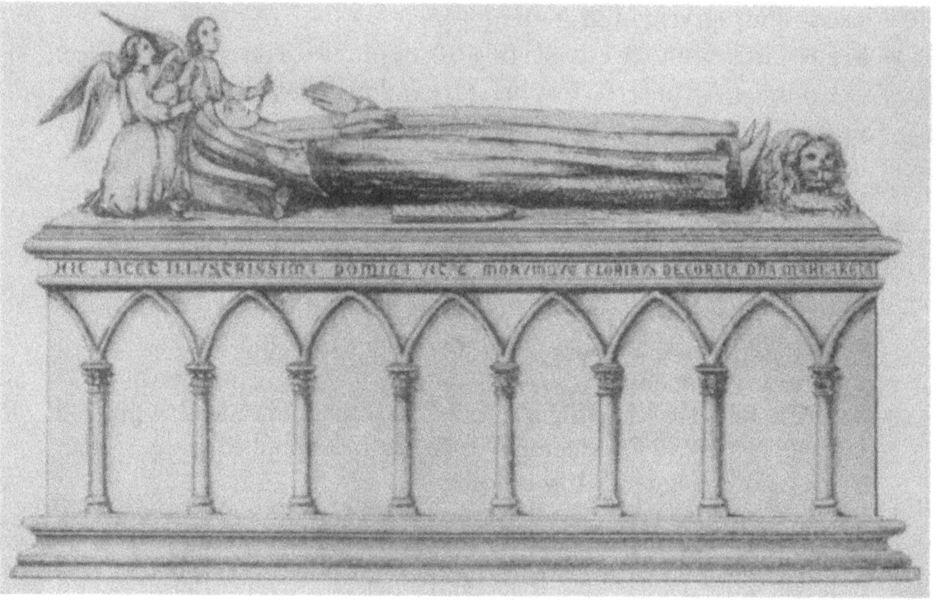

Fig. 55. Tonnerre. Tomb of Marguerite de Bourgogne (lost). (After Petit)

[20] See pp. 4-5 above. The quote is an unbiased assessment by Joseph Strayer, *The Reign of Philip the Fair* (Princeton: 1980) p. 207.

[21] The inscription on her tomb (Fig. 55) was published by Luyt, *La Princesse* (1653) pp. 87-88 and many times since: Le Maistre (1867) p. 90; Dormois, "Description" p. 186; Petit, "Archives" p. 32; Edmond Renault, "Les Tombes de l'église de l'hôpital des Fontenilles à Tonnerre" *Annuaire historique et statistique du département de l'Yonne* 50e année (2e série v. 25) (1886) pp. 204-5. All authors state that the tomb was destroyed in 1793; it was replaced in 1826 by a new one of different design. However, the 1890 catalog of the Musée de Troyes lists a "statue de Marguerite de Bourgogne, qui se trouvait sur son tombeau à l'hôpital de Tonnerre - XIIIe s.," a copper *gisant* which was purchased in 1874 from the estate of L. Coutant: Louis Le Clert, *Musée de Troyes. Archéologie monumentale. Catalogue* (Troyes: 1890) p. 97 no. 480. In a 1997 letter to me the museum stated that the statue is no longer in its possession.

APPENDIX I
THE FABULOUS GENEALOGY AND HERALDRY OF PERE JACQUES VIGNIER

The Jesuit father Jacques Vignier (1603-69) wrote works on the region in which he lived and on his family's history, and his interest in Mussy-sur-Seine derived from the coats of arms he saw in the church that were related, though not identical, to the heraldry used by the family in his lifetime. One cannot charge him with reticence or even logic in the pursuit of historical truth; Langres, he maintains, was built shortly after Noah's Flood and the 'temerity of Babylon.'[1] Though his writing abounds in casual error and in hasty unexamined connections, the fascination of its endless continuum of names, dates and authoritative assertions has often seduced modern historians like Roserot and Bautier. In this study I have struggled to avoid reliance on Vignier, but like historians before me—where his detail happens to fit into the picture that is emerging—have occasionally succumbed. I always, however, have indicated Vignier as the source when no other witness exists. Even Branner allowed that tradition is not always wrong.

Jacques Vignier S.J. collected endless materials for a history of the diocese of Langres, now Paris, BNF fr. 5993-5998. A résumé of his labors was composed, translated into Latin, and published during his lifetime under the title *Chronicon lingonense* (Langres: 1665). In 1842 Emile Jolibois edited and translated this text into French, adding a continuation up to 1792: *Les Chroniques de l'évêché de Langres* (Chaumont: 1842) 287 pp. An edited version of selections from the Vignier materials of general regional interest, prepared either by himself or another and now preserved as BNF fr. 18717-18718, was finally published by the Société historique et archéologique de Langres with an informative introduction

[1] Jacques Vignier, *Chronicon lingonense* (Langres: 1665) p. 1; Jolibois translation pp. 3-4. On these publications see below.

concerning the man and his work: Jacques Vignier, *Décade historique du diocèse de Langres* (Langres: 1891-94) 2 vols. Publication of the six volumes of manuscript notes (BNF fr. 5993-5998) is unlikely ever to be undertaken. As hinted with extreme sangfroid by the professional archivists responsible for the 1890s edition, Vignier's manuscripts are in tiny, crabby handwriting, faded, smeared, ink-blotted, scratched out, with additions and corrections jamming the margins and between the lines, the pages torn, chewed, bearing the marks of many aborted pagination systems—in other words, seventeenth-century clutter at its worst. While I have checked Bautier's and Lambert's citations from the manuscript volumes and have corrected the latter's page citation to conform to the more correct foliation, I have left it at that.

Even before the Latin précis appeared in 1665, Vignier's manuscript was used as a source by Nicolas de La Brosse, *Description de la terre et baronnie de Ricey*, published in the same volume following Pierre Dubreuil, *Histoire ample des peuples habitans aux trois bourgs de Ricey* (Paris: 1654). Dubreuil paraphrased Caesar to make a case for a presumed Roman colonization of Les Riceys; de La Brosse is chiefly useful for his detailed description of the sixteenth/seventeenth-century château of Ricey-Bas, then owned by the Vignier family. The rooms were decorated with heraldry of various alleged ancestors and their marriage alliances. On p. 105 de La Brosse begins a long *Arbre généalogique de la maison de Vignier* starting with the troubadour Gilles le Vinier (fl. 1240), repeating Vignier's "identification" of him at Mussy (see below).[2] The works of Debrueil and de La Brosse were produced to buttress the attempt by Louis Vignier to get his baronny of Les Riceys raised to a marquisate, which succeeded in 1669: "On doit se mettre en garde contre les bévues

[2] De La Brosse also published the integral text of a 1646 manuscript entitled "Généalogie des seigneurs de Ricey, depuis l'an 1086 jusqu'à l'an 1646, tirée de plusieurs chartes, titres et papiers, qui sont ès abbeyes de Molesme, de Saint-Pierre-le-Vif de Sens, de Mores, et de divers contrats ..., par Charles Vignier, escuyer, demeurant à Bar-sur-Seine" (now BNF fr. 5995 fols. 242-47). See Roserot, *Dictionnaire* III p. 1255f. Jacques Vignier evidently was not the only member of his clan fascinated by the romance of genealogy. For more scientifically based information on the early seigneurs de Ricey see the genealogical chart in Jacques Laurent, "A propos de l'ascendance maternelle de saint Bernard. Seigneurs de Montbard et seigneurs de Ricey," *Mélanges saint Bernard*, 24e Congrès de l'Association bourguignonne des sociétés savantes, 1953 (Dijon: 1954) following p. 13.

et les hyperboles évidemment dictées aux auteurs par le désir de plaire au seigneur châtelain [Vignier]."[3]

Roussel has provided an excellent warning in approaching the work of Jacques Vignier:[4]

> On peut considerer le Père Jacques Vignier, homme savant, habile et laborieux, comme un peintre un peu complaisant, qui s'applique à embellir ses portraits pour les rendre plus agréables....On peut encore reprocher à Jacques Vignier un certain amour pour le merveilleux, un certain penchant pour établir des sentiments nouveaux, sans chercher à les appuyer par les raisons solides et convaincantes....Cette hardiesse de l'auteur à faire passer pour des vérités incontestables des opinion très-controversées, se montre moins dans son *Chronicon* que dans ses manuscrits....Nous voulons seulement prévenir le lecteur de se montrer circonspect et de ne pas accueillir légèrement toutes les assertions de l'auteur.
>
> (One can consider Père Jacques Vignier—a man learned, adroit and hard-working--like a rather fawning painter who applies himself to beautify his portraits in order to make them more agreeable.... One can further reproach in Jacques Vignier a certain love of the marvelous, a certain penchant to assert new opinions without attempting to support them by solid and convincing proof....This audacity of the author in allowing controversial opinion to pass for incontestable truth is less evident in his *Chronicon* than in his manuscripts.... We only wish to warn the reader to be circumspect and not to entertain lightly all the assertions of the author.)

Vignier had found in the publication of Claude Fauchet, *Recueil de l'origine de la langue et poësie françoise* (1581, 2nd ed. 1610), among a list of 127 medieval poets, the names of two thirteenth-century *trouvères* called messire Gilles le Viniers and maître Guillaume le Viniers, 'perhaps his brother or cousin.'[5] The few poetic lines Fauchet quoted from Messire

[3] Alexandre Guénin and Alexandre Ray, "Statistique de canton des Riceys," *Mémoires de la Société académique d'agriculture, des sciences, arts et belles-lettres du département de l'Aube* XVI (2e série v. III) (1851-52), pp. 619-20. See also Charles-Ludovic Ray, *Une Légende pour rire concernant les Riceys* (Arcis-sur-Aube: 1914) pp. 3-5.

[4] Roussel, *Le Diocèse de Langres* IV p. 247.

[5] Claude Fauchet (1530-1601), *Recueil de l'origine de la langue et poésie françois, ryme et romans, plus les noms et sommaires des oeuvres de CXXVII poètes françois, vivans avant l'an*

Gilles mention his going to Syria. In attempting to construct a family genealogy on this flimsy foundation, and to connect it to the medieval heraldry he saw at Mussy, Vignier concocted the following confused and baseless assertion (BNF fr. 5994 fol. 270v):[6]

> L'ayeul de Gilles Vignier, Guillaume Vignier ou le Vinier fut vivant entre l'an 1200 et 1240. Gilles, qualifié messire, fut en la terre sainte, l'an 1238, avec le duc de Bourgogne et le comte de Champagne, Thibault, roi de Navarre, et autres princes; et en retourna vers l'an 1240, laissa lignée et fut enterré en l'église collègiale de Mussy. On voit qu'il a été fondateur, que ses armes étaient celles qui se voient aux clefs de la voûte, et que l'effigie du chevalier qui est représenté dans les vitres avec sa cotte d'armes, et sur sa sépulture qui est dans le choeur à côté du grand autel, est la sienne. Toutefois, il y a sujet d'un doute, vu que c'est le blason de ceux du surnom de Mussy, un peu différent de l'escu de la branche de Vignier.
>
> (The kinsman of Gilles Vignier, Guillaume Vignier or le Vinier lived ca. 1200-40. Gilles, called *messire*, was in the Holy Land in 1238 with the duke of Burgundy and the count of Champagne, Thibault, king of Navarre, and other princes; and, returning around 1240, left progeny and was buried in the collegiate church of Mussy. One sees that he was founder, that his arms were those on the vault keystones, and that the image of the knight appearing in the windows in his heraldic surcoat, and on his tomb in the choir beside the main altar, is his. However there is cause for doubt, since it is the heraldry of those surnamed de Mussy, a little different from the arms of the branch of Vignier.)

He adds on fol 272r, providing a small misleading sketch:[7]

M.CCC (Paris: 1581) Book II p. 149 no. LI (Gilles le Viniers) and p. 183 no. CIIII (Guilleaume le Viniers). The microfilm in the BNF is missing pp. 182-83. Vignier's use of Fauchet is criticized in Charles-Ludovic Ray, *Le Père Jacques Vignier, généalogiste de sa lignée* (Troyes: 1921) pp. 9-12; Ray, *Légende* p. 15; Lambert pp. 350-54.

[6] Lambert published these texts pp. 353-54. For "ancestor" Gilles Vinier see also BNF fr. 5995 fol. 599v. I have discussed Vignier's blazon of the Mussy arms on p. 52 above.

[7] It is misleading since it is labeled 'H. de Mussy 1373' but must have been made from his seal, to which Vignier attributed the tinctures he found in the examples at Mussy. On the tinctures used by Henri de Mussy, see p. 47 above.

"les armes des de Mussy sont de gueules au chef d'or, à la bande componée de sable et d'argent de six pièces...."

And in the next volume (BNF fr. 5995 fol. 220r) he adds unhelpfully:[8]

(L)es armes des de Mussy semblent celles qui sont au château de Chesley, au pied de la croix de pierre du village ..., d'or à un chef de gueules, à la bande componée d'argent et de sable de huit pièces qui sont les mêmes que celles de Vignier....

De La Brosse's publication of 1654, which reached a larger audience, summarized selected passages from the above without any qualifying 'sujet d'un doute,' unaware—or perhaps ignoring—that in the same volume (BNF fr. 5995 fol. 247v) Vignier had changed his mind again and placed the tomb of Gilles le Vinier elsewhere, in the church of Lisle-en-Bourgogne.[9]

The Vignier family only came into possession of the château at Ricey—and perhaps to their pretensions to grandeur?—in 1622,[10] and there seems to be no evidence that their heraldry predates that era. Seventeenth-century armorials give their arms as *d'or au chef de gueules à la bande componée d'argent et de sable brochant sur le tout*, that is, identical to the fourteenth-century arms of the branch of the de Mussy family established at Chesley and Chaource (and differenced from the de Mussy arms in the stained glass of Mussy-sur-Seine).[11] Following 1650 the Vignier were allowed by royal concession to add to their arms a border of *France ancien* (*azur semée de fleurs de lis d'or*), and these arms were adopted shortly thereafter by the town of Les Riceys, of which the

---

[8] Vignier's manuscript also contains a small sketch here, showing arms quarterly (1) Monstier, (2) Mussy, (3 and 4) blank, dated 1569.

[9] Lambert p. 354. De La Brosse invents, as seigneur of Lisle, 'Humbert de Mussy, Gilles' son,' alive in 1280 and making a will 1320: Ray, *Légende* p. 14; Lambert p. 352.

[10] Roserot, *Dictionnaire* III p. 1258; Guénin and Ray p. 588; Charles Lalore, "Reciacus, Les Riceys (Aube)," *Mémoires de la Société académique d'agriculture, des sciences, arts et belles-lettres du département de l'Aube* XXXVI (1872) p. 180.

[11] See discussion, pp. 46-51 above. For the Vignier arms see Louvan Geliot, *La Vraie et parfaite science des armoiries, augm. par Pierre Palliot*, II (1660, facsimile ed. Paris: 1895) p. 669.

Vignier were at that moment the seigneurs.[12]

My own hypothesis about the origin of the Vignier arms, which I cannot prove, is that the aggressively upward-mobile family assumed as their arms ca. 1620 heraldry they found displayed on one of their newly acquired properties. The canton of Les Riceys (See Fig. 1) lies between the canton of Mussy on one side and the canton of Chaource on the other,[13] and in Chaource a branch of the de Mussy was well-established by the mid fourteenth century, using the arms later appropriated by Vignier (Figs. 31-32). The de Mussy and Monstier families of Chaource intermarried by ca. 1400 and the latter often quartered the arms of both (Fig. 30). For example, Jean du Monstier (d. 1419) and his son Jean (d. 1483) owned land at Les Riceys, and their arms, quartering (1 and 4) Monstier with (2 and 3) de Mussy, appear in a fresco at Chaource, accompanied by their kneeling images and an inscription giving their names and the dates of death.[14]

Père Vignier solved the vexing problem of why his imaginary thirteenth-century ancestor Gilles le Vinier, supposedly memorialized at Mussy-sur-Seine, had different arms from the seventeenth-century arms of Vignier, by inventing another fable concerning an earlier branching of the family. A Vignier, he posits, in 1086 before going on the First Crusade, sold the main part of Mussy to the count of Tonnerre, while his cadet brother remained in town as seigneur of a lesser part and took the

[12] The post-1650 arms of Vignier appear in Louis-François de Caumartin, *Procez verbal de la recherche de la noblesse de Champagne* (Châlons: 1673, rpt. Paris: 1982) p. 122; Raoul de Warren, *Grand armorial de France* VI (Paris: 1949, rpt. 1975) p. 458 (arms of families registered in 1696). Warren notes that the family seems to have been ennobled in 1418. The border of *France* later grows so large that the Vignier arms form a mere inescutcheon in the center: Jacques Chevillard, *Armorial de Bourgogne et de Bresse* (Paris: 1728) fol. 7; Chevillard, *Nobiliare de Champagne et de Brie* (Paris: 1758, rpt. 1978) fol. II-4. On the arms of the town of Les Riceys: Gildas Bernard, *Armorial des communes du département de l'Aube*,10, Tome 1: *Chefs-lieux de canton* (Troyes: 1959) unpaginated.

[13] Guénin and Ray p. 534.

[14] On the fresco: Marc Thibout, "La Peinture murale de l'église de Chaource," *Congrès archéologique* CXIII (1955) pp. 371-72; Ernest Petit, "Voyage de l'Abbé Lebeuf à Clairvaux en 1730," *Bulletin de la Société des sciences historiques et naturelles de l'Yonne* XLI (1887)p. 40. On the Monstier at Les Riceys: Roserot, *Dictionnaire* I pp. 317, 382, and III p. 1257; Guénin and Ray p. 589.

name 'de Mussy.'[15] The arms of the two branches of the family were thus appropriately differenced and his own family of Vignier was the main line. This interpretation of the arms borne by the Vignier in the seventeenth century has survived in heraldic works such as that of Le Clert, reprinted as recently as 1976,[16] without the least basis in fact.

Are we not in the world of Stendhal's Marquise de La Mole?:[17] 'She makes it no secret that to have had ancestors who went to the Crusades is the sole advantage to which she attaches any importance.'

---

[15] Roserot, *Dictionnaire* II p. 1009.

[16] Louis Le Clert, *Armorial historique de l'Aube* (1911, rpt. Marseille: 1976) p. 312. The logic of chronology compelled Le Clert to suggest that the medieval de Mussy family was probably the main line and the seventeenth-century Vignier, a cadet branch.

[17] *Le Rouge et le Noir* Livre II ch. I.

APPENDIX II

TONNERRE: THE WOODEN STATUES AND THE QUEEN'S "COMPANIONS"

Two wood, formerly polychromed, statues of standing women survive at Tonnerre.[1] A third one, matching them, is commonly assumed to have been lost, although there is no evidence that it ever existed. The style of the existing pair places them generally around 1300. They have long been associated with the queen of Sicily and two aristocratic 'companions in residence,' Catherine de Courtenay and Marguerite de Beaumont. In Salet's opinion the most likely identifications are the queen and Marguerite de Beaumont since, as he notes, both headdresses cover the neck, inappropriate for a young unmarried (or recently married) woman such as Catherine.[2]

In reality the residences of both Catherine and of Marguerite de Beaumont at Tonnerre were much less significant than has been assumed. Catherine appears in the obituary of Tonnerre with an *anniversarium duplex*, and in the cartulary as the founder of a chapel dedicated to her name-saint in March 1301, by which time she was the wife of the king's brother Charles de Valois.[3] She was the granddaughter of Charles d'Anjou, born and raised at his court (and that of Marguerite de Bourgogne) in Naples, with her cousins the children of Charles II d'Anjou. Catherine was born in 1274 and her mother, Béatrix de Sicilie (Charles' daughter by his first wife), died when she was aged one. Her father Philippe de Courtenay, titular emperor of Constantinople, had no other

[1] Claude Schaefer, *La Sculpture en ronde-bosse au XIVe siècle dans le duché de Bourgogne* (Paris: 1954) pp. 85, 176, pl. 51b. Illustrations: Quénée figs. 29, 30; Skórka and Fontaine (as in Part III n. 31) p. 29 (color details).

[2] Salet, "Tonnerre" p. 234. On such headdresses see p. 60 above. The statues are identified on postcards at the Musée de Tonnerre as Catherine(?) and the queen. Le Maistre (1867) p. 83, thought they were Catherine and Marguerite de Beaumont. Ernest Petit identified the slimmer one as Catherine and illustrated it in "Statue de sainte Catherine à l'hôpital de Tonnerre," *Bulletin de la Société des sciences historiques et naturelles de l'Yonne* (1910) pp. 5-7. They are presumed to be the queen and Marguerite de Beaumont in *L'Art au temps des rois maudits* p. 119.

[3] Petit, "Archives," pp. 14-15, 30.

children and died in 1284, a year before Charles did.

Thus when the widowed queen of Sicily, Marguerite de Bourgogne, left southern Italy for France in 1285, Catherine was twenty-one years of age and an orphan, whose empty title of empress of Constantinople made her much sought after. She remained in residence at the court of Naples until Philippe le Bel sent for her in May 1294, and she promised to obtain the assent of her uncle Charles II d'Anjou for any proposed marriage. While she undoubtedly visited Marguerite de Bourgogne once she was in France, she did not reside at Tonnerre but at the court of Philippe le Bel in Paris as far as we know. In the spring of 1299, for example, she was with Robert d'Artois and his countess at Bapaume, Beuvry, Aire, Hesdin, Tournehem, Merck and Calais. After a succession of aborted marriage arrangements, she was wed to Philippe le Bel's recently widowed brother Charles de Valois in February 1301. She bore four children before dying in childbirth 1307, and was buried at the Jacobins in Paris.[4]

Marguerite de Beaumont also has an *anniversarium duplex* in the Tonnerre obituary, mentioning only her gift of a vineyard; in the cartulary this gift is dated 1299 and designated for her anniversary.[5] Around 1304 she founded a chapel in the hospital, dedicated to the Trinity. In the 1305 testament of the queen of Sicily, Marguerite de Beaumont is named as one of the executors.[6]

Marguerite de Beaumont was princess of Antioch—by then an empty title—and countess of Tripoli. She was a cousin of Catherine of Courtenay's father, and is often called a kinswoman of the queen of Sicily, though as far as I can tell they were not related by blood but only through the marriage alliance of Catherine's parents.[7] While Marguerite de Beaumont was a granddaughter of John of Brienne, king of Jerusalem, and married through his agency to Bohemond VII, prince of Antioch and count of Tripoli, she had

[4] On Catherine de Courtenay see: Pierre Bony, "Le Gisant en marbre noir de Saint-Denis: les signes symboliques de l'emperatrice Marie de Brienne?," *Revue française d'héraldique et de sigillographie* nos. 54-59 (1984-89) p. 95 and tableau I after p. 110; Gaston Sirjean, *Encyclopédie généalogique des maisons souveraines du monde, Branches cadettes* v. I no. XI. *Les Courtenay* (Paris: 1966) p. 171; Georges Digard, *Philippe le Bel et le Saint-Siège de 1285 à 1304* (Paris: 1936) I pp. 191, 225 and II p. 21; Joseph Petit, *Charles de Valois (1270-1325)* (Paris: 1900) pp. 53-56; Le Maistre (1867) pp. 78-81; Anselme I p. 101.

[5] Petit, "Archives" pp. 18, 30; Le Maistre (1867) p. 82.

[6] Petit, "Histoire" VI no. 5800; Le Maistre (1867) pp. 87-88.

[7] On Marguerite de Beaumont: Du Cange, *Les Familles d'outremer*, ed. Emmanuel-Guillaume Rey (Paris: 1869) p. 486; Le Maistre (1867) pp. 81-83; Anselme II p. 594, VI p. 137. See Le Maistre p. 109 for her kinship with Catherine de Courtenay.

been born in western France in the Maine. Her parents, Louis de Brienne-Beaumont and Agnes de Beaumont, were married before 1250, and Marguerite was married to Bohemond by 1277.[8] They had no children, and lived in Tripoli where he died in 1287. In March 1289 the Arabs besieged and took Tripoli and Marguerite and Bohemond's sister Lucie escaped.[9] Since Lucie was the wife of Narzonus de Toucy, who served Charles d'Anjou in high military and administrative office, the two women probably went to the court of Naples. Marguerite de Bourgogne had by this time returned to France.

When Marguerite de Beaumont arrived in France is uncertain, but in the years around 1290 and beyond, her mother was still living in western France as were her brother and two sisters, all with large families. She undoubtedly had gone to live at Tonnerre with Queen Marguerite by 1299, date of her gift of the vineyard. In the queen's 1305 testament, she left a book of hours "a la princesse d'Antioche, qui demoure auecque moi."[10]

Marguerite de Beaumont seems to have moved from Tonnerre upon the death of her friend in 1308; letters from her dated 1312 and 1322 are in the cartulary, where her own testament of 1328 appears sealed by the *châtelain* of Pontoise.[11] She probably went to the Cistercian nunnery of Maubuisson (Seine-et-Oise, arr. Pontoise), where her family had strong connections. The abbess Blanche de Brienne (d. 1309) was her cousin; at least two of her nieces were nuns; and the church housed the tombs of her aunt, uncle and grandmother. Upon her death in 1328, she too was buried there—and not at Tonnerre as often stated. Her tomb was destroyed in 1793.[12]

In my opinion, while no firm identifications are possible, the most likely hypothesis is that neither statue represents the queen of Sicily. Both Catherine de Courtenay and Marguerite de Beaumont were honored at Tonnerre as founders of chapels. The statues are of wood, thus unlike the hospital's luxurious fittings and more probably commissioned after the death of the

---

[8] In 1277 Bohemond did homage to Charles d'Anjou, through an agent, for his county of Tripoli; Marguerite de Beaumont, in the same year, ceded to Charles her claims on the kingdom of Jerusalem. Le Maistre (1867) pp. 81-82; Anselme II p. 594.

[9] Digard I pp. 74-75. On Narzonus de Toucy (d. 1292 in Naples): Du Cange pp. 487-88; Paul Durrieu, *Les Archives angevines de Naples* II (Paris: 1887) p. 390; Petit, *Histoire* VI p. 40.

[10] Le Maistre (1867) p. 83.

[11] Petit, "Archives," p. 17.

[12] Bony, "Le Gisant" p. 92, tableau II; Du Cange p. 486.

queen of Sicily in 1308. Once her magnificent tomb with its crowned and gilt effigy was installed in the choir, the community may have decided to add wooden statues of the founders of the chapels — in which case they represent Catherine of Courtenay and Marguerite of Beaumont. The fact that one of the figures has a veiled head with marks indicating a crown would not have been inappropriate for either, Marguerite de Beaumont being entitled princess of Antioch while Catherine, married to a French prince, remained empress of Constantinople.

SELECTED BIBLIOGRAPHY

ADHÉMAR, JEAN, "Les Tombeaux de la collection Gaignières," *Gazette des beaux-arts* Pt I, CXVI (6e période v. LXXXIV)(1974) pp. 1-192; Pt II, CXVIII (6e période v. LXXXVIII)(1976) pp. 89-128; Pt III, CXIX (6e période v. XC) (1977) pp. 1-76.

AMÉ, EMILE, *Les Carrelages émaillés du moyen-âge et de la Renaissance* (Paris: 1859).

ANSELME, PÈRE, *Histoire de la maison royale de France et des grands officiers de la couronne*, 3rd rev. ed. (1726-33, rpt. 1967) 8 vols.

ARNAUD, ANNE-FRANÇOIS, *Voyage archéologique et pittoresque dans le département de l'Aube* (Troyes: 1837).

L'Art au temps des rois maudits, Philippe le Bel et ses fils 1285-1328, exh. Cat. Grand Palais (Paris: 1998).

BARTHÉLEMY, ANATOLE DE, "Une Monnaie inédite de Langres," *Bulletin de la Société historique et archéologique de Langres* I (1880) pp. 266-70.

BARTHÉLEMY, EDOUARD DE, ed., *Voyage littéraire de Dom Guiton en Champagne (1744-1749)* (Paris: 1889).

BAUTIER, ROBERT-HENRI, "Guillaume de Mussy, bailli, enquêteur royal, pannetier de France sous Philippe le Bel," *Bibliothèque de l'Ecole des chartes* CV (1944) pp. 64-98. (Reprinted in Bautier, *Etudes sur la France capétienne: De Louis VI aux fils de Philippe le Bel*, Variorum CS 359 [Aldershot, Hants: 1992]).

BEAU, ANNICK, and ANDRÉ MATTON, "Iconographie tonnerroise, Vitraux du vieil hôpital représentant les portraits de Marguerite de Bourgogne et de son époux Charles Ier d'Anjou," *Bulletin de la Société d'archéologie et d'histoire du Tonnerrois* no. 26 (1973) pp. 51-55.

BELOTTE, MICHEL, "Les Possessions des évêques de Langres dans la région de Mussy-sur-Seine et de Châtillon-sur-Seine du milieu du XIIe au milieu du XIVe siècle," *Annales de Bourgogne* XXXVII no. 147 (Jul-Sept 1965) pp. 161-97.

BROWN, ELIZABETH A. R., "The Prince is Father of the King: The Character and Childhood of Philip the Fair of France," *Mediaeval Studies* XLIX (1987) pp. 282-334. (Reprinted in Brown, *The Monarchy of Capetian France and Royal Ceremonial*, Variorum CS 345 [Aldershot, Hants: 1991]).

COTHREN, MICHAEL, "The Thirteenth- and Fourteenth-Century Glazing in the Choir of the Cathedral of Beauvais," Ph.D. dissertation Columbia 1980.

COULON, AUGUSTE, *Inventaire des sceaux de la Bourgogne* (Paris: 1912).

DAGUIN, ARTHUR, "Les Evêques de Langres, étude épigraphique, sigillographique et héraldique," *Mémoires de la Société historique et archéologique de Langres* III (1880) pp. 1-188.

DORMOIS, CAMILLE, "Description des bâtiments de l'hôpital de Tonnerre," *Bulletin de la Société des sciences historiques et naturelles de l'Yonne* VI (1852) pp. 177-89.

DOUËT-D'ARCQ, LOUIS, *Collection de sceaux* II (Paris: 1867, rpt. Munich: 1980).

DURRIEU, PAUL, *Les Archives angevines de Naples, étude sur les registres du roi Charles Ier (1265-1285)* (Paris: 1886) 2 vols.

GATOUILLAT, FRANÇOISE, "Vitreries de type cistercien dans l'Yonne," in *Archéologie, histoire et folklore du nord de l'Yonne*, Actes du 56e Congrès de l'Association bourguignonne des sociétés savantes (Villeneuve-sur-Yonne: 1985) pp. 59-64.

LALORE, CHARLES, *Etat de la paroise de Chaource avant la Révolution* (Arcis-sur-Aube: 1884).

LAMBERT, CHARLES-AUGUSTE-JOSEPH, *Histoire de la ville de Mussy-L'Evêque (Aube)* (Chaumont: 1878).

LANGLOIS, CHARLES-VICTOR, *Le Règne de Philippe III le hardi* (Paris: 1887).

LE CLERT, LOUIS, *Armorial historique de l'Aube* (1911, rpt. Marseille: 1976).

LE MAISTRE, LOUIS, "Marguerite de Bourgogne, reine de Naples, de Sicile et de Jérusalem, comtesse de Tonnerre," *Annuaire historique du département de l'Yonne* (1867) pp. 43-109.

LE MAISTRE, LOUIS, "Sur les sceaux de Marguerite de Bourgogne, comtesse de Tonnerre, reine de Naples, de Sicile et de Jérusalem," *Recueil des travaux de la Société de sphragistique de Paris* II (1852-53) pp. 141-51.

LILLICH, MEREDITH PARSONS, *The Armor of Light: Stained Glass in Western France, 1250-1325* (Berkeley: 1994).

———, "Early Heraldry: How to Crack the Code," *Gesta* XXX/1 (1991) pp. 41-47.

———, "European Stained Glass around 1300: The Introduction of Silver Stain," *Europäische Kunst um 1300* VI/6, Akten des XXV. Internationalen Kongresses für Kunstgeschichte, 1983 (Vienna: 1986) pp. 45-60, 287-90.

———,"Heraldry and Patronage in the Lost Windows of Saint-Nicaise de Reims," *L'Art et les révolutions* VIII, 27e Congrès international d'histoire de l'art, 1989 (Strasbourg: 1992) pp. 71-102.

———, "Monastic Stained Glass: Patronage and Style," in *Monasticism and the Arts*, ed. Timothy Verdon (Syracuse: 1984) pp. 207-54.

———, *Rainbow Like an Emerald: Stained Glass in Lorraine in the Thirteenth and Early Fourteenth Centuries* (University Park, Pa: 1991).

———, "Recent Scholarship Concerning Cistercian Windows," in *Studiosorum Speculum: Studies in Honor of Louis J. Lekai, O.Cist.*, ed. Francis Swietek and John Sommerfeldt (Kalamazoo: 1993) pp. 233-62.

———, *The Stained Glass of Saint-Père de Chartres* (Middletown, Conn.: 1978).

———, "Three Essays on French Thirteenth Century Grisaille Glass," *Journal of Glass Studies* XV (1973) pp. 69-78 .

LONGNON, AUGUSTE, *Documents relatifs au comté de Champagne et de Brie, 1172-1361* II, III (Paris: 1901-14).

LUYT, ROBERT, *La Princesse charitable et aulmoniere, ou l'histoire de la reyne Marguerite de Bourgongne, comtesse de Tonnerre...* (Troyes: 1653, rpt. Tonnerre: 1979).

MATHIEU, JEAN-BAPTISTE-JOSEPH, *Abrégé chronologique de l'histoire des évêques de Langres*, 2nd ed. (Langres: 1844).

PETIT, ERNEST, "Archives de l'hôpital de Tonnerre. Le cartulaire. L'obituaire," *Bulletin historique et philologique du Comité des travaux historiques et scientifiques* (1906) pp. 10-32.

———, *Histoire des ducs de Bourgogne de la race capétienne* (Dijon: 1898).

PINTO, ANNE, "Les Vitraux de l'abside de Mussy-sur-Seine," Mémoire de maîtrise, Université de Paris IV, 1985.

PRINET, MAX, "Armoiries françaises et allemandes décrites dans un ancien rôle d'armes anglais," *Le Moyen âge* XXXIV (1923) pp. 223-60.

———, "L'Armorial de Bourgogne du Héraut Berry," *Le Moyen âge* 3e série v. II (1931) pp. 161-219.

———, "Armorial de France composé à la fin du XIIIe siècle ou au commencement du XIVe," *Le Moyen âge* XXXI (1920) pp. 1-49.

———, "Sceaux franc-comptois décrits dans un ouvrage de sigillographie dauphinoise,"*Académie des sciences, belles-lettres et arts de Besançon, Procès-verbaux et Mémoires* [unnumbered] (1907) pp. 146-63.

QUARRÉ, PIERRE, "Les Statues de la Vierge à l'Enfant des confins burgondo-champenois au début du XIVe siècle," *Gazette des beaux-arts* CX (6e période v. LXXI) (1968) pp. 193-204.

QUÉNÉE, NOËL, *L'Hôpital Notre Dame des Fontenilles à Tonnerre*, 2nd ed. (La Pierre-qui-Vire: 1979).

RAGUIN, VIRGINIA, *Stained Glass in Thirteenth-Century Burgundy* (Princeton: 1982).

RAY, CHARLES-LUDOVIC, *Le Père Jacques Vignier, généalogiste de sa lignée* (Troyes: 1921).

Recensement III = *Les Vitraux de Bourgogne, Franche-Comté et Rhône-Alpes*, Corpus Vitrearum France, Recensement III (Paris: 1986).

Recensement IV = *Les Vitraux de Champagne-Ardenne*, Corpus Vitrearum France, Recensement IV (Paris: 1992).

RICHARD, JEAN, *Les Ducs de Bourgogne et la formation du duché de XIe au XIVe siècle* (Paris: 1954).

ROGER, JEAN-MARC, "Les Morhier champenois," *Bulletin philologique et historique (jusqu'à 1610) du Comité des travaux historique et scientifique* VII (1978) pp. 77-130.

Rolls of Arms, Henry III, Aspilogia II (London: 1967).

ROSEROT, ALPHONSE, *Dictionnaire historique de la Champagne méridionale (Aube) des origines à 1790* (Langres/Troyes: 1942, rept. Marseille: 1983-84) 3 vols.

ROUSSEL, CHARLES-FRANÇOIS, *Le Diocèse de Langres, histoire et statistique* (Langres: 1873) 4 vols.

SALET, FRANCIS, "L'Eglise de Mussy-sur-Seine," *Congrès archéologique* CXIII (1955) pp. 320-37.

———, "L'Hôpital Notre-Dame des Fontenilles à Tonnerre," *Congrès archéologique* CXVI (1958) pp. 225-39.

SCHMOLL GEN. EISENWERTH, JOSEF ADOLF, "Die Madonna von Bayel (Südchampagne) und ihre Schlüsselrolle für die Lothringische Skulptur des frühen 14. Jahrhunderts," *Wiener Jahrbuch für Kunstgeschichte* XLVI/XLVII t. 2 (1993-94) pp. 641-56.

THIBOUT, MARC, "La Peinture murale de l'église de Chaource," *Congrès archéologique* CXIII (1955) pp. 370-74.

VIGNIER, JACQUES, *Décade historique du diocèse de Langres* (Langres: 1894).

Les Vitraux de Bourgogne...: see Recensement III.

Les Vitraux de Champagne-Ardenne: see Recensement IV.

ZAKIN, HELEN, *French Cistercian Grisaille* (New York: 1979).

GENERAL INDEX

[A separate Index of Monuments and Works of Art follows this General Index]

INDEX OF MONUMENTS AND WORKS OF ART

www.ingramcontent.com/pod-product-compliance
Lightning Source LLC
LaVergne TN
LVHW081603100826
845153LV00004B/445
9780871698834